Bioterrorism

Other Books of Related Interest

Opposing Viewpoints Series

Biological Warfare

At Issue Series

Weapons of War

Current Controversies Series

Biodiversity

"Congress shall make
no law … abridging
the freedom of speech,
or of the press."

First Amendment to the US Constitution

The basic foundation of our democracy is the First Amendment guarantee of freedom of expression. The Opposing Viewpoints Series is dedicated to the concept of this basic freedom and the idea that it is more important to practice it than to enshrine it.

I Bioterrorism

Roman Espejo, Book Editor

GREENHAVEN PRESS
A part of Gale, Cengage Learning

GALE
CENGAGE Learning

Detroit • New York • San Francisco • New Haven, Conn • Waterville, Maine • London

Elizabeth Des Chenes, *Director, Publishing Solutions*

© 2013 Greenhaven Press, a part of Gale, Cengage Learning

Gale and Greenhaven Press are registered trademarks used herein under license.

For more information, contact:
Greenhaven Press
27500 Drake Rd.
Farmington Hills, MI 48331-3535
Or you can visit our Internet site at gale.cengage.com.

For product information and technology assistance, contact us at:

Gale Customer Support, 1-800-877-4253.
For permission to use material from this text or product, submit all requests online at www.cengage.com/permissions.

Further permissions questions can be emailed to permissionrequest@cengage.com.

Articles in Greenhaven Press anthologies are often edited for length to meet page requirements. In addition, original titles of these works are changed to clearly present the main thesis and to explicitly indicate the author's opinion. Every effort is made to ensure that Greenhaven Press accurately reflects the original intent of the authors. Every effort has been made to trace the owners of copyrighted material.

Cover image © Hemera/Thinkstock/Getty Images.

LIBRARY OF CONGRESS CATALOGING-IN-PUBLICATION DATA

Bioterrorism / Roman Espejo, book editor.
   p. cm. -- (Opposing viewpoints)
   Includes bibliographical references and index.
   ISBN 978-0-7377-6474-1 (hardcover) -- ISBN 978-0-7377-6475-8 (pbk.)
   1. Bioterrorism. 2. Bioterrorism--United States--Prevention. 3. Agriculture--Defense measures--United States. I. Espejo, Roman, 1977-
   HV6433.3.B567 2012
   363.325'30973--dc23
                        2012019754

Printed in the United States of America
1 2 3 4 5 6 7 16 15 14 13 12

Contents

Chapter 3: How Should the United States Prepare for and Protect Against Bioterrorism?

Chapter 4: What Anti-Bioterrorism Policies Should the United States Have?

Why Consider Opposing Viewpoints?

> "The only way in which a human being
> can make some approach to knowing
> the whole of a subject is by hearing
> what can be said about it by persons of
> every variety of opinion and studying
> all modes in which it can be looked at
> by every character of mind. No wise
> man ever acquired his wisdom in any
> mode but this."
>
> *John Stuart Mill*

In our media-intensive culture it is not difficult to find differing opinions. Thousands of newspapers and magazines and dozens of radio and television talk shows resound with differing points of view. The difficulty lies in deciding which opinion to agree with and which "experts" seem the most credible. The more inundated we become with differing opinions and claims, the more essential it is to hone critical reading and thinking skills to evaluate these ideas. Opposing Viewpoints books address this problem directly by presenting stimulating debates that can be used to enhance and teach these skills. The varied opinions contained in each book examine many different aspects of a single issue. While examining these conveniently edited opposing views, readers can develop critical thinking skills such as the ability to compare and contrast authors' credibility, facts, argumentation styles, use of persuasive techniques, and other stylistic tools. In short, the Opposing Viewpoints Series is an ideal way to attain the higher-level thinking and reading skills so essential in a culture of diverse and contradictory opinions.

In addition to providing a tool for critical thinking, Opposing Viewpoints books challenge readers to question their own strongly held opinions and assumptions. Most people form their opinions on the basis of upbringing, peer pressure, and personal, cultural, or professional bias. By reading carefully balanced opposing views, readers must directly confront new ideas as well as the opinions of those with whom they disagree. This is not to argue simplistically that everyone who reads opposing views will—or should—change his or her opinion. Instead, the series enhances readers' understanding of their own views by encouraging confrontation with opposing ideas. Careful examination of others' views can lead to the readers' understanding of the logical inconsistencies in their own opinions, perspective on why they hold an opinion, and the consideration of the possibility that their opinion requires further evaluation.

Evaluating Other Opinions

To ensure that this type of examination occurs, Opposing Viewpoints books present all types of opinions. Prominent spokespeople on different sides of each issue as well as well-known professionals from many disciplines challenge the reader. An additional goal of the series is to provide a forum for other, less known, or even unpopular viewpoints. The opinion of an ordinary person who has had to make the decision to cut off life support from a terminally ill relative, for example, may be just as valuable and provide just as much insight as a medical ethicist's professional opinion. The editors have two additional purposes in including these less known views. One, the editors encourage readers to respect others' opinions—even when not enhanced by professional credibility. It is only by reading or listening to and objectively evaluating others' ideas that one can determine whether they are worthy of consideration. Two, the inclusion of such viewpoints encourages the important critical thinking skill of objectively evaluating an author's credentials and bias. This evaluation will illuminate an author's reasons for taking a particular stance on an issue and will aid in readers' evaluation of the author's ideas.

It is our hope that these books will give readers a deeper understanding of the issues debated and an appreciation of the complexity of even seemingly simple issues when good and honest people disagree. This awareness is particularly important in a democratic society such as ours in which people enter into public debate to determine the common good. Those with whom one disagrees should not be regarded as enemies but rather as people whose views deserve careful examination and may shed light on one's own.

Thomas Jefferson once said that "difference of opinion leads to inquiry, and inquiry to truth." Jefferson, a broadly educated man, argued that "if a nation expects to be ignorant and free . . . it expects what never was and never will be." As individuals and as a nation, it is imperative that we consider the opinions of others and examine them with skill and discernment. The Opposing Viewpoints Series is intended to help readers achieve this goal.

David L. Bender and Bruno Leone,
Founders

Introduction

*"If the destruction is delayed
indefinitely, the synthesis and
preparation of smallpox virus as a
bioweapon by a non-superpower would
increase, and it may truly become a
poor man's atom bomb."*

Kalyan Banarjee, former director
of the National Institute of
Virology.

*"Secure virus stocks in the United States
and Russia may still prove useful and
should not be destroyed. A political
compromise is the best way to make
that happen."*

Nature.

Smallpox, the first disease to be eliminated by medical science, was declared eradicated in 1980 after mass vaccinations. Part of the pox family, the disease is caused by the variola virus, which can be spread through the air or contact with contaminated objects and skin lesions of the infected. It is characterized by flu-like symptoms and a flat rash that appears after the fever subsides, erupting into painful pustules that feel like hard, tiny pellets embedded in the skin. The fatality rate was 1 percent in its less common form (variola minor) and 30 percent in its more common form (variola major). Deaths also resulted from bacterial infections, pneumonia, and other complications. Other than treating sores and easing pain for patients, the disease had no treatments, and survivors were left with disfiguring pockmarks from the pustules. Widely feared, smallpox killed between 300 million to 500 million people in the twentieth century alone.

In the United States, the last case of smallpox occurred in 1949, and routine vaccinations concluded in 1972. As for the rest of the world, the last natural occurrence was seen in 1977 in Somalia. However, a year later, a medical photographer was exposed to the virus at a British university research laboratory, killing her and sickening her mother. After this incident, stocks of smallpox were either destroyed or transferred to two high-containment facilities located in the United States and Russia. In 1986, routine vaccinations ceased globally, and the World Health Organization (WHO) recommended that remaining samples be destroyed, which was postponed several times throughout the 1990s and 2000s.

While the chance of another accidental exposure exists at the high-containment facilities, numerous experts have greater fears that the virus will fall into the hands of terrorists or rogue states. The use of smallpox as a biological weapon has been documented several times in modern history. During the French and Indian War, the British allegedly gave infected blankets to Native Americans, whose populations were decimated by the disease due to their lack of immunity. In addition, during the Revolutionary War, the British purportedly deployed immunized civilians to spread smallpox among US forces in Montreal, afflicting half of the ten thousand soldiers. British, American, and Japanese scientists later researched the virus as a biological warfare agent during World War II, but widespread vaccinations limited interest in it as a weapon.

In a series of revelations, it became known that the former Soviet Union made significant advances in the weaponization of smallpox. In 1992, Ken Alibek, a Kazakh scientist who defected from the nation and served as first deputy director of biowarfare facility Biopreparat, claims that the Soviet Union did not shelve its program like the United States and United Kingdom. "A real turning point was when I came to the US and I saw all the so-called BW [biowarfare] facilities, completely abandoned, not active. I was shocked," he says. According to him, the Soviets elected to modify a highly virulent strain, India 67 or India 1, and created methods to mass produce the virus. Alibek reports that they had hundreds of metric tons of smallpox stockpiled and developed capabilities to disperse it with missile warheads and aerial bombing. He is concerned that after the dissolution of the Soviet Union, samples were sold in secret and jobless researchers headed to illicit laboratories that weaponized smallpox. Some intelligence reports indicate that Iran and North Korea presently have the abilities to launch such a strike.

In 2011, the WHO's decision-making body, the World Health Assembly (WHA), postponed its discussion to set a destruction date for the remaining smallpox stocks until 2014. The joint resolution proposed by the United States and Russia to continue smallpox research until 2016 was supported by Canada, Australia, and the European Union, but opposed by WHO's Eastern Mediterranean region, China, Indonesia, and other countries. Proponents of preserving the virus maintain that the development of smallpox vaccinations remains vital to global health and security. "Destruction of the last securely stored viruses is an irrevocable action that should occur only when the global community has eliminated the threat of smallpox once and for all. To do any less keeps future generations at risk from the reemergence of one of the deadliest diseases humanity has ever known," contends Kathleen Sebelius, secretary of the US Department of Health and Human Services. On the other hand, opponents persist that not only does storage of samples put the world in jeopardy of the disease's return, the virus is no longer useful to research. "Destroying smallpox virus stocks is not only the last step in the great achievement of eradicating the disease, it is the single most important thing that the international community can do to ensure that it never appears again," declares an open letter to the WHA undersigned by forty civil society organizations across the globe. "By making possession of the virus a crime against humanity, any future attempt to recreate the virus through biotechnology methods would meet international condemnation and sanction."

The engineering of the smallpox virus for warfare is but one of the issues at the forefront of the biosecurity debate. Threats to the food supply, the proliferation of high-containment laboratories, and the United States' preparedness for a bioterrorist attack challenge defense experts, public health administrators, scientists, and activists. *Opposing Viewpoints: Bioterrorism* probes these topics and more in the following chapters: How Great Is the Threat of Bioterrorism?, What Are the Issues Associated with Biodefense Research?, How Should the United States Prepare for and Protect Against Bioterrorism?, and What Anti-Bioterrorism Policies Should the United States Have? The divided arguments and analyses in this volume attest to the devastating possibilities and controversial unknowns of biological weapons.

OPPOSING
VIEWPOINTS®
SERIES

CHAPTER 1

How Great Is the Threat of Bioterrorism?

Chapter Preface

At the Seventh Review Conference of the Biological Weapons Convention in December 2011, US Secretary of State Hillary Clinton warned of the "evolving" problem of bioterrorism. "The advances in science and technology make it possible to both prevent and cure more diseases, but also easier for states and non-state actors to develop biological weapons," Clinton stated. "A crude, but effective, terrorist weapon can be made by using a small sample of any number of widely available pathogens, inexpensive equipment, and college-level chemistry and biology." Clinton spoke of the role of genetics in the development of harmful agents. "The emerging gene synthesis industry is making genetic material widely available. This obviously has many benefits for research, but it could also potentially be used to assemble the components of a deadly organism," she explained.

However, the position that genetics heighten the threat of biological weapons has not reached a total consensus in the defense community. "Some believe that, inevitably, these advances will lead to a catastrophic biological attack. Others believe that, despite these advances, the scientific and technical requirements, as well as the fundamental laws of natural selection will prevent such an attack," observes the National Defense University's Center for Technology and National Security Policy (CTNSP) in a May 2011 paper.

In the center's view, a non-state actor may not have the technological capabilities and means to launch such an assault. "Further development of a modified pathogen for use in a full-scale direct catastrophic biological attack is feasible, but the full spectrum of technologies for scale-up, testing, packaging, weapon production, and employment will most likely require the resources of a nation-state or comparably resourced organization," the CTNSP contends. In the following chapter, authors analyze the current state of biological terrorism.

"Naturally occurring disease remains a serious biological threat; however, a thinking enemy armed with these same pathogens—or with multi-drug-resistant or synthetically engineered pathogens—could produce catastrophic consequences."

Bioterrorism Poses a Serious Threat

The Bipartisan WMD Terrorism Research Center

In the following viewpoint, the Bipartisan WMD Terrorism Research Center contends that the United States is increasingly vulnerable to bioterrorist attacks. It maintains that small groups with graduate-level training can produce deadly, drug-resistant pathogens using equipment easily acquired through the Internet. Even more disconcerting is that rapid technological advancement will enable these groups to engineer and release more devastating pathogens in the coming years according to the WMD Center. Prevention efforts alone will not guarantee safety from bioterrorist attacks, it warns. Founded in 2010, the WMD Center is a nonprofit, nonpartisan research and education organization focused on the study of weapons of mass destruction.

As you read, consider the following questions:
1. According to the WMD Center, what surprise emerged from a 1999 study on the production of biological weapons?
2. How does the WMD Center describe the aerosolization of a bioweapon?
3. Why is deterrence against nonstate actors largely ineffective, in the WMD Center's view?

There is no question America is vulnerable to infectious and contagious diseases. The influenza pandemic of 1918–1919 killed more than 20 million people—more than 600,000 in the United States. That winter, more U.S. soldiers died from influenza than had died on World War I battlefields.

According to Centers for Disease Control and Prevention (CDC), nearly 40,000 Americans die annually from seasonal flu. And most experts agree that the human race is long overdue for an influenza pandemic far more deadly than the H1N1 pandemic of 2009–2010. However, the threat from Mother Nature goes far beyond the flu.

An average of 15–20 previously unknown diseases have been discovered in each of the past few decades—including incurable diseases like HIV/AIDS, Ebola, hepatitis C, Lyme disease, hantavirus pulmonary syndrome, and Severe Acute Respiratory Syndrome (SARS). Studies indicate that new strains of influenza and other newly emerging diseases are likely to spread even more broadly and quickly due to the mobility of the world's population. Additionally, many of the diseases once managed with medical countermeasures are now re-emerging in strains resistant to drug therapies. And modern technology threatens to speed the development of such novel diseases and enhance the threat they pose to the population at large.

The emergence of such a deadly pandemic, for which the nation was unprepared to respond, could change America forever.

Naturally occurring disease remains a serious biological threat; however, a thinking enemy armed with these same pathogens—or with multi-drug-resistant or synthetically engineered pathogens—could produce catastrophic consequences.

A National Security Perspective

The relative threat of bioterrorism has been intensely debated within the national security community for more than a decade, with a focus on the biotech revolution and which capabilities fall within the reach of non-state actors.

In many respects, this debate is reminiscent of previous national security arguments. Shortly after World War I, two junior Army officers began writing articles in military journals about high-speed tanks and how they could revolutionize land warfare. Their ingenuity was severely chastised by the Commander of the Infantry in the War Department. He threatened the young officers with charges of insubordination if they continued to advocate high-speed tanks. The senior officer stated, "There is no reason for a tank to ever exceed three miles per hour, because that is the fastest an infantry unit can move on a battlefield."

Thankfully, Major George S. Patton and Captain Dwight D. Eisenhower were undeterred by the warnings from the War Department. They continued their research and advocacy because they were convinced we could not predict the future by looking to the past.

During World War I, the technology was not available to produce high-speed tanks, so few really considered the possibility of massive armored juggernauts moving at high speed out in front of the infantry. However, on September 1, 1939, 2,400 German tanks raced across the Polish border, far in advance of German infantry units. The armored columns were supported by another rapidly emerging technology—airpower—and a new concept of warfare was introduced: Blitzkrieg (lightening war).

Some national security technologies require decades to mature, such as tanks and airplanes; others require far less time. In

June 1941, the U.S. Navy concluded that Pearl Harbor was too shallow for the effective use of air-dropped torpedoes. This was a correct assessment for June 1941. But in September 1941, the Japanese Navy discovered that simple wooden boxes attached to the rear of torpedoes would allow them to operate in shallow water. On December 7, 1941, 27 of these newly modified torpedoes struck U.S. warships in Pearl Harbor.

Assessing the Threat

Today, some scholars would look to the past to predict the future of bioterrorism. They argue it has proven too difficult for terrorist groups to successfully develop and use sophisticated bioweapons—that the threat is overstated.

A better way to forecast the threat of bioterrorism is by careful examination of three critical questions:

- Can non-state actors produce and deliver biological weapons? (Capability)
- Is there a desire by terrorists to use biological weapons? (Intent)
- Would using biological weapons produce the intended effects? (Vulnerability and Consequences)

Capability

When the Biological Weapons Convention (BWC) was ratified in 1972, the ability of nation-states to produce sophisticated bioweapons was unquestioned. These weapons were capable of killing on the scale of nuclear weapons, but compared to the cost of a nuclear weapons program, they were far less expensive—hence the term, "poor-man's atom bomb."

There was little or no consideration of non-state actors producing such weapons in the 1970s. That changed, however, by the end of the century. Dr. George Poste, then chairman of the Defense Science Board, predicted, "In terms of national security, the 20th century will be remembered as the century of physics, but the 21st century will be remembered as the century of biology."

The first piece of hard evidence regarding the capability of non-state actors to produce sophisticated biological weapons came in 1999 from a [U.S. Department of Defense] Defense Threat Reduction Agency study called Biotechnology Activity Characterization by Unconventional Signature (BACUS). The initial purpose of the study was to determine if a small-scale bio-weapons production facility would produce an observable "intelligence signature."

The answer was no. The study concluded that even when using "national technical means," it would be extremely difficult, if not impossible, for the intelligence community to detect a clandestine production facility. This conclusion was somewhat expected. The surprise, however, came from an experiment conducted as part of the study. Individuals with no background in the development and production of bioweapons and no access to the classified information from the former U.S. bioweapons program were able to produce a significant quantity of high-quality weaponized *Bacillus globigii*—a close cousin to the well-known threat, Anthrax.

In spring 2001, the Defense Science Board (DSB) released a report, co-authored by Nobel Laureate Dr. Joshua Lederberg and the former chair of the chemistry department at Harvard, Dr. George Whitesides, entitled Biological Defense. The report stated:

> Major impediments to the development of biological weapons —strain availability, weaponization technology, and delivery technology—have been largely eliminated in the last decade by the rapid global spread of biotechnology.

Unbeknownst to the authors of the DSB report, al Qaeda had already begun its bioweapons programs in Afghanistan and Malaysia in late 1999 under the supervision of Ayman al Zawahiri. (Zawahiri is now the leader of al Qaeda.)

Although many initially assumed the anthrax letters of October 2001 came from al Qaeda, the Federal Bureau of Investigation (FBI) is now convinced the anthrax letters came from a U.S. Army civilian employee at Ft. Detrick, Maryland.

This conclusion remains controversial. If the FBI is correct, however, then a single individual with no work experience in the weaponization of pathogens (a vaccine specialist), using equipment that could readily be purchased over the Internet, was able to produce very high-quality, dry-powdered anthrax.

Fortunately, the casualties were limited (22 infected and five died) because the small quantity of material was delivered with warning notes inside the envelopes. But according to Dr. Peggy Hamburg, the current FDA Administrator, an attack releasing the same quantity of dry-powdered anthrax into the ventilation system of the World Trade Center in late August 2001, could have killed far more people than the airplane attacks did on 9/11.

The FBI theory of the attacks is that a single individual, working alone late at night, produced enough dry-powder anthrax to mount the attacks through the mail. A small team could have used the same approach to create enough product to attack a city.

Despite advances in biotechnology, some skeptics continue to ask where terrorists could obtain such pathogens. Unfortunately, most pathogens likely to be used as weapons exist widely in nature. Anyone seeking to develop these pathogens as weapons would not have to look far for sources.

Clearly then, small, disaffected, but technically competent groups could develop credible biothreats to the United States. The next question is whether they could deliver it.

There are three primary means of delivering a bioweapon:

• Putting it in food or water,

• Using vectors (such as fleas, ticks, or infected humans), or

• Pumping it into the air (aerosolization).

All of these approaches are possible, but the most effective method is aerosol release.

The aerosolization of pathogens was perfected during the Cold War by U.S. and Soviet military scientists. Releasing pathogens in 3–5 micron size allows them to enter the lungs and flow immediately into the blood stream. In the 1960s, achieving this effect required sophisticated technology available only to major nation-states. Today, pulmonary drug delivery is used worldwide by the medical and pharmaceutical industries.

In summary, modern biotechnology provides small groups the capabilities for a game-changing bio-attack previously reserved to nation-states. Even more troubling, rapid advances in biotechnology, such as synthetic biology, will allow small teams of individuals to produce increasingly powerful bioweapons in the future.

Intent

Critics who question whether terrorists intend to develop and use bioweapons should consider the following:

- The Aum Shinrikyo cult in Japan attempted to produce both anthrax and botulinum toxin weapons. In 1995 they released large quantities of non-pathogenic *Bacillus anthracis* in Tokyo.

- A January 2010 Belfer Center Study on Terrorism and WMD [Weapons of Mass Destruction] by Rolf Mowat-Larssen observed:

  Another 9/11-scale operational plot managed by the al Qaeda core leadership was the development of anthrax for use in a mass casualty attack in the United States. The sophisticated anthrax project was run personally by al Qaeda deputy chief Ayman al Zawahiri, in parallel to the group's efforts to acquire a nuclear capability; anthrax was probably meant to serve as another means to achieve the same effect as using a nuclear bomb, given doubts that a nuclear option could be successfully procured. Notably, al Qaeda's efforts to acquire nuclear and biological weapons capability were concentrated in the years preceding

September 11, 2001. Based on the timing and nature of their WMD-related activity in the 1990s, al Qaeda presumably anticipated using these means of mass destruction against targets in the U.S. homeland in the intensified campaign they knew would follow the 9/11 attack. There is no indication that the fundamental objectives that lie behind their WMD intent have changed over time.

- A video played worldwide on al Jazeera TV in February 2009 featured a Kuwaiti professor talking about bringing four pounds of dry-powdered anthrax to Washington, D.C., and killing several hundred thousand Americans. It has been viewed more than 100,000 times on various web sites.

- The web site of Anders Behring Breivik, the perpetrator of the 2011 terrorist attacks in Norway, talked of using anthrax weapons. There is serious doubt that he had the technical capability to produce any type of bioweapon, but little question he would have used one if available. Clearly, one should not assume that international terrorists are the sole threat for bioterrorism. Had Ted Kaczynski (the Unabomber) been a microbiologist rather than a mathematician, he might have selected a far more deadly form of weapon.

Vulnerability and Consequences

Despite major improvements in public health and medical science, the human race remains vulnerable to infectious diseases. A global economy and highly mobile population make the likelihood and consequences of a disease outbreak even greater. In 2003, a single individual infected with the SARS virus spread the disease to 24 people—who in three days, had traveled to six countries on four continents.

With respect to man-made threats, this vulnerability is also clear. The offensive bioweapons programs of the United States and the former Soviet Union demonstrated, without question, the potential lethality of sophisticated bioweapons.

But 40 years of advancement in biotechnology may now enable development of bioweapons by small nation-states and non-state actors. This growing threat creates significant new vulnerabilities for our nation and the world, as described by President Obama in a foreword to the National Security Council's Strategy for Countering Biological Threats:

> The effective dissemination of a lethal biological agent within an unprotected population could place at risk the lives of hundreds of thousands of people. The unmitigated consequences of such an event could overwhelm our public health capabilities, potentially causing an untold number of deaths. The economic cost could exceed one trillion dollars for each such incident. In addition, there could be significant societal and political consequences that would derive from the incident's direct impact on our way of life and the public's trust in government.

Consider, for example, smallpox—a disease that killed more than 300 million people in the 20th century. Although it was eradicated in its natural form 30 years ago, concerns remain that someone might still hold stores that could have a devastating effect on unvaccinated populations today. Even worse, the causative agent, variola virus, can be synthetically produced in high-tech laboratories. Should the government prove unprepared for either a natural outbreak or an attack, the consequences might shake the very foundations of America.

As technology spreads, the growing challenge of attribution may also make us even more vulnerable than in the past.

Until now, the combination of the Biological Weapons Convention and traditional deterrence has prevented nation-state use of bioweapons. But, deterrence is largely ineffective against non-state actors because they are hard to find and hold accountable. Should rogue nation-states provide sophisticated bioweapons to non-state actors, while remaining "a silent partner" to bioterrorism, the problem would be compounded.

The threat of biological disaster is real and growing. There are people in this world with the capability and the intent to use biological weapons. Americans are vulnerable to such an attack, as we are to a naturally occurring disease pandemic. The consequences of either could harm the fabric of the nation itself.

> *"Advances in the life sciences may gradually put bioweapon capabilities closer within terrorist reach, but scientific and technological progress alone doesn't warrant exaggeration of the bioterrorist threat."*

Biological Threats: A Matter of Balance

The Scientists Working Group on Biological and Chemical Weapons

In the following viewpoint, the Scientists Working Group on Biological and Chemical Weapons asserts that the threat of bioterrorism is distorted. Proposed scenarios that forecast large-scale catastrophes are based on unrealistic measures and ignore the difficulties of effectively deploying bioweapons, the Working Group states. As political attention and financial resources have been directed toward bioterrorism, it adds, little progress has been made in the preparedness against infectious diseases and food-borne illnesses. Aimed against the misuse of biology, the Working Group was founded in 1989 by the Federation of American Scientists and joined the Center for Arms Control and Non-Proliferation in 2003.

As you read, consider the following questions:

1. How does the Working Group view the 2001 anthrax letter attacks?
2. What mortality figures does the Working Group provide to back the urgency of other public health needs?
3. What has resulted from the expansion of biodefense research, as claimed by the Working Group?

The Graham-Talent WMD Commission asserted again last week that a bioterrorism attack that "will fundamentally change the character of life for the world's democracies" is highly likely to occur within the next four years. The commission argues that the United States must urgently expand its efforts to develop vaccines and other medical countermeasures against potential bioterrorism agents.

We disagree with the commission on both points. It exaggerates the bioterrorist threat and proposes solutions that won't produce the comprehensive approach needed to strengthen public health security.

The bioterrorist threat must be kept in perspective. Although many fictional "tabletop" scenarios and exercises have predicted bioterrorism catastrophes, these scenarios often have used unrealistic values for critical disease parameters and have routinely ignored the organizational and technical difficulties that terrorists would have in organizing, and successfully carrying out, a bioweapons attack. The history of both state-operated bioweapons programs and unsuccessful terrorist attempts to develop and use such weapons (e.g., the Japanese cult Aum Shinrikyo) have demonstrated, again and again, the significant difficulties that confront making and disseminating a biological weapon. The 2001 anthrax letter attacks, which were seen as validating the catastrophic scenarios, appear to have been executed with anthrax developed in a U.S. biodefense laboratory with capabilities vastly superior in scale and quality to anything a terrorist could achieve.

Advances in the life sciences may gradually put bioweapon capabilities closer within terrorist reach, but scientific and technological progress alone doesn't warrant exaggeration of the bioterrorist threat. Rather than basing policy on worst-case scenarios, the United States should develop and conduct more plausible, sophisticated threat assessments that take into account the complex set of political, social, and technical factors that would affect bioweapons development and use.

Since the 2001 anthrax attacks, the federal government has spent nearly $60 billion responding to the perceived threat of bioterrorism. Roughly one-half of that money has funded detection systems, dramatically expanded research on bioweapon agents, and the development, procurement, and stockpiling of vaccines and other medical countermeasures against these agents.

As bioterrorism has commanded policy and funding attention over the last decade, domestic influenza-related deaths have likely exceed 300,000 people. The growing problem of multi-drug resistant tuberculosis, the lack of progress on reducing food-borne infections and disease outbreaks, and annual U.S. mortality figures from AIDS (14,000 deaths) and opportunistic infections such as MRSA (19,000 deaths) all speak to significant ongoing public health needs. Policy and funding decisions must be based on more than just mortality statistics. For instance, government is expected to respond effectively to acute disease outbreaks. Nonetheless, these figures underscore that continuing to emphasize and spend billions of dollars on measures to specifically counter exaggerated bioterrorist threats diverts attention and resources from other pressing natural disease threats and public health concerns.

Moreover, all the money and effort spent on biodefense hasn't produced demonstrably better overall health security for the country. Detection systems remain unreliable triggers for immediate responses. Expansion of biodefense research has increased the number of people with access to dangerous

An Impact out of Proportion

The increased threat of terrorism necessitates an evaluation of the risk posed by various microorganisms as biological weapons. This is especially important in the case of the filoviruses, Marburg and Ebola, both because these agents pose a threat as lethal pathogens and because their use by terrorists might result in extreme fear and panic. Most of the public knowledge of these viruses is based on inaccurate and exaggerated accounts in popular books and movies. If terrorists were to cause even a few Ebola or Marburg infections in a number of cities, public perception of a threat of epidemic spread could cause major social and economic disruption. A limited attack might thus achieve an impact out of proportion to the actual number of illnesses and deaths. . . .

If an aerosol attack with a filovirus goes undetected, at least a week will elapse before the onset of the first illnesses. By that time, no infectious virus will remain in the environment, and there will be no need for surface decontamination. Even if an attack is detected while still in progress, or is discovered soon after completion through law enforcement investigation, persons who have not actually inhaled the agent will be at negligible risk of infection from any residual aerosolized virus that might linger in the environment, since the few viral particles that might adhere to skin, clothing or surfaces would degrade within hours through the action of UV light. However, as in all biowarfare situations, it would be prudent for people who may have been exposed to an aerosolized agent to take a full body shower with soap and to wash their clothing in hot water with detergent.

Mike Bray, "Defense Against Filoviruses Used as Biological Weapons," Antiviral Research, *vol. 57, January 2003.*

pathogens and toxins, which increases the risk of accidents, infiltration by outside groups, or attack by a rogue insider. Programs to develop stockpiles of vaccines against bioweapon agents continue to face questions relating to efficacy, safety, shelf life, and timely distribution. Many other bioweapon-specific countermeasures will be useless against serious infectious disease problems, other acute public health threats, or even bioterrorist attacks that differ from the threat predicted. Despite promises of broad-based "synergies," most of these efforts haven't produced benefits for public health, as illustrated by the problems experienced in the responses to pandemic influenza A (H1N1).

Nonetheless, the Graham-Talent Commission wants U.S. policy makers to continue down this questionable path with more urgency, more money, and more intense focus on bioterrorist threats. Such an approach will exacerbate the political and funding gaps between defense against bioterrorism and protection of the U.S. population from naturally occurring infectious diseases. Strangely, the Commission points to the H1N1 pandemic as evidence that the United States should devote more funding to biodefense, when the proper conclusion to draw from the troubles experienced with H1N1 is that Washington isn't paying enough attention to public health capabilities in its efforts to strengthen national health security.

Rather than continuing to argue, despite accumulated evidence to the contrary, that bioterrorism-centric policy and spending will produce meaningful and sustainable positive "spillover" effects for public health, a better, more comprehensive approach to national health security would focus on improving public health capabilities to respond to any kind of infectious disease threat. As the recently released U.S. National Health Security Strategy states, "Investments should focus, to the extent possible, on new technologies and countermeasures that could also have uses in non-public health emergency situations."

This more comprehensive approach would focus political attention and fiscal resources on addressing important public health and national health security needs, including:

- Ensuring that the nation's public health system is capable of addressing all public health needs, including infectious disease outbreaks. Only by ensuring adequate staffing and resources in all program areas will the United States build a sustainable public health system that can strengthen individual resistance to disease, improve early detection and treatment, and contain disease outbreaks, whether natural, deliberate or accidental.

- Increasing support for the basic tools necessary for public health surveillance and epidemiology, including skilled personnel, public health laboratories, and data collection, management, analytic, and information-sharing systems. In this respect, the roughly $15 billion in biodefense spending to strengthen state and local public health capacity and fund other public health efforts *has* been important and needs to be maintained and even enhanced.

- Enhancing animal disease surveillance and response capabilities and their integration with public health systems, which would improve the ability to rapidly detect and diagnose both animal and zoonotic infections and disease outbreaks, whether natural or deliberate.

- Improving disaster preparedness and response capabilities, especially medical surge capacity. The capabilities needed to respond quickly and effectively to an event that produces a large number of casualties are similar whether the event is a natural disease outbreak, a bioterrorism event, or a natural disaster such as an earthquake or tsunami.

- Strengthening research on new diagnostics, antibiotics, and antivirals for emerging or established diseases that cause significant mortality or morbidity. An ability to more rapidly develop, test, and verify the safety of new vaccines after an epidemic or pandemic is also important. However, emergency-response strategies shouldn't overly focus on vaccination because vaccines usually need to be given prior to exposure. New vaccines will continue to take time to produce, and stockpiled vaccines are highly disease-specific (often even strain-specific) and often have a limited shelf life.

Public health in the United States faces many challenges; bioterrorism is just one. Policies need to be crafted to respond to the full range of infectious disease threats and critical public health challenges rather than be disproportionately weighted in favor of defense against an exaggerated threat of bioterrorism. Nine years after the anthrax letters, we know better than to expect narrowly construed biodefense policies to produce comprehensive health security for the U.S. people.

"*Protecting the U.S. food supply from intentional adulteration has grown in importance since the attacks of September 11, 2001.*"

Bioterrorism Threatens Food Supplies

Office of the Inspector General, US Department of Homeland Security

In the following viewpoint, the Office of the Inspector General (OIG) maintains that bioterrorism poses numerous hazards to the nation's food supply. A large-scale event of contamination, the OIG claims, is a growing concern in light of unintentional outbreaks of foodborne illnesses that affect large populations; experts speculate that deliberate outbreaks can be more devastating and result in shortages of certain products. Also, the OIG suggests that food supply attacks can disrupt essential services of state and local governments and weaken the public's confidence in the food industry and related institutions. The OIG is an independent body that investigates and audits the programs and personnel of the US Department of Homeland Security.

Office of the Inspector General, US Department of Homeland Security, "Background," *The Department of Homeland Security's Role in Food Defense and Critical Infrastructure Protection*, February 2007, pp. 2–5, 7–8.

As you read, consider the following questions:

1. What did the President's Council of Advisors state about terrorist attacks on the food supply?
2. How can the widespread outbreak of a communicable disease affect the food sector, as claimed by the OIG?
3. As described by the OIG, how many Americans could be poisoned by one gram of botulinum type A toxin?

The nation's food sector is comprised of an array of distinct businesses and operations that help bring food products to consumers around the world. The host of steps in the food production system is often collectively described as a "farm-to-table" continuum. This continuum is, in fact, a tremendously complex system characterized by numerous interdependencies. . . .

Pre-harvest elements of the continuum include crops and animals in the field, as well as fertilizers and animal feed. The harvesting or slaughter of agricultural products marks the beginning of the post-harvest food sector, which extends through the balance of the continuum until products are consumed. This review concentrated on post-harvest elements of the food supply so as not to duplicate previous Government Accountability Office work on the pre-harvest side.

The post-harvest food industry accounts for 12% of the nation's economic activity and employs more than 10% of the American workforce. It consists of enormous subsectors, including business lines addressing processing, storage, transportation, retail, and food service. Statistics on just two of these subsectors serve to illustrate the magnitude of the sector.

The National Restaurant Association projects that the industry's 925,000 U.S. locations will reach $511 billion in sales for 2006, serving over 70 billion "meal and snack occasions" for the year. Meanwhile, the nation's $460 billion food retail business consists of more than 34,000 supermarkets, 13,000 smaller food markets, 1,000 wholesale club stores, 13,000 convenience stores, and 28,000 gas station food outlets. Like the other components of the food industry, these subsector business units have a broad geographic distribution and are present in all regions of the country.

Private sector entities are the predominant owners and operators of the food sector. Federal, state, and local governments have noteworthy food production, distribution, retail, and service operations, but these are small when compared to private sector operations.

Regulation of the food industry is divided between federal, state, and local agencies. State, territorial, and local governments conduct oversight of food retail and food service establishments within their jurisdictions. These levels of government oversee restaurants, institutional food service establishments, and hundreds of thousands of food retailers. Within the federal government, primary responsibility for food safety rests with two agencies. The Food Safety and Inspections Service of the U.S. Department of Agriculture (USDA) oversees the processing of red meat, poultry, and processed egg products. The Food and Drug Administration (FDA) of the Department of Health and Human Services (HHS), in turn, regulates the processing of virtually all other food products. In addition to these two, several other federal agencies provide oversight of food processing, distribution, and retail. . . .

Hazards to the Food Sector

The food sector could experience several types of significant adverse events. Among these, intentional food contamination is of greatest concern to many in the food security and safety fields. In December 2004, the former Secretary of Health and Human Services, Tommy Thompson remarked that, "I, for the life of me, cannot understand why the terrorists have not attacked our food supply because it is so easy to do."

Protecting the U.S. food supply from intentional adulteration has grown in importance since the attacks of September 11,

Contamination of Water Supplies

Deliberate contamination of domestic water supplies with a biological agent is feasible. However, there are a number of barriers to its effectiveness: dilution, inactivation by chlorine treatment, or ozone treatment, filtration and the relatively small quantity of water that each person drinks. Nevertheless, the protozoan *Crytosporidium parvum* can persist through these barriers. This is evident from the 1993 outbreak in Milwaukee where 403,000 people developed cryptosporidiosis. At least 54 people died, and 4,400 were hospitalised. Obviously, poorly mainlined water treatment plants pose a great threat to the risk of waterborne diseases through accidental and deliberate contamination. The contamination of food processors water supply could be even more detrimental through subsequent economic losses or product recall, as well as the number of illnesses. The international recall of 160 million bottles of sparkling bottled water due to possible benzene contamination in 1990 well illustrates this point.

Stephen J. Forsythe, The Microbiology of
Safe Food. *Ames, IA: Blackwell Publishing,*
2010.

2001. Some have suggested that terrorist attacks on the food supply are increasingly likely. In 2003, the President's Council of Advisors on Science and Technology wrote that "terrorist acts of a widely diffuse nature such as attacks on the food supply . . . could become a preferred means of attack in an environment where terrorist networks have been 'decapitated' and their ability to communicate and raise funds significantly diminished." Food products may be deliberately contaminated with chemical, biological, or radiological agents. Despite the range of possible contaminating agents and the openness of parts of the food supply chain, there have been few recorded cases of deliberate food contamination in the United States. These events have only had a localized effect and have not resulted in serious casualties on a massive scale or catastrophic economic loss. The following are three prominent domestic incidents of food contamination:

- In 1984, members of a religious cult poisoned ten Oregon salad bars with *Salmonella*, resulting in 751 individual cases of illness.

- In 1996, a disgruntled employee of a Texas hospital willfully tainted snacks in a staff break room. This incident caused illness in 12 people.

- In 2003, a Michigan supermarket employee infected 200 pounds of beef with an insecticide, causing illness in 92 people.

Though it is without domestic precedent, the prospect of a mass-scale food contamination event is of particular concern because the nation is subject to major *unintentional* foodborne illness outbreaks. Experts reason that, with some study and limited access, an individual or individuals with malevolent aims could reproduce these outbreaks with more dire consequences. In 2003, the FDA wrote that, "If an unintentional contamination of one food . . . can affect 300,000 individuals, a concerted, deliberate attack on food could be devastating, especially if a more dangerous chemical, biological, or radionuclear agent were used."

Food safety practitioners devote considerable attention and resources to addressing the hazards associated with *unintentional* food contamination. In the past, this type of food contamination has led to some major outbreaks, which have occurred with much more frequency and on a considerably larger scale than deliberate acts of contamination. In 1985, for example, the unintentional contamination of milk with *Salmonella typhimurium* caused illness in 170,000 individuals in the United States. A decade later, an estimated 224,000 people in

41 states became ill after consuming ice cream with *Salmonella enteriditidis.*

While foodborne disease outbreaks typically result from products contaminated by naturally occurring biological pathogens, foodborne illnesses have also been traced to toxins, heavy metals, pesticides, and other chemicals. In 1981, for instance, a toxic agent in cooking oil sickened about 20,000 and resulted in the deaths of approximately 800 in Spain. Such contamination events can have long-term effects. In Michigan in 1973, a fire retardant containing a potentially carcinogenic hazardous substance was inadvertently mixed with cattle feed and several thousand people ingested products from animals that had eaten the contaminated feed. Studies have shown that people who consumed these products maintained high levels of the toxic substance years later. It persists, for example, in the breast milk of women who consumed affected foods.

Shortages and Disruptions

Intentional or unintentional damage to food industry facilities could also adversely affect the sector and result in temporary shortages of certain food products. Because there are available substitutes for most foodstuffs, however, the effect of such losses may be firm-, product-, or industry-specific, and not widespread. Damage to facilities at "chokepoints" in the supply chain for a number of food products, however, could have more pronounced economic effects.

The food sector could also suffer adversely from the debilitation of other sectors. Because food is often consumed some distance from its point of production, significant transportation disruptions have the potential to spawn food shortages. The availability of food products is also dependent on the continuing efforts of the food sector workforce. Conditions that undermine the willingness of food industry workers to go to their worksites or to otherwise perform their jobs could also contribute to food shortages. Because major U.S. cities typically have access to about one week's supply of food, however, transportation and labor disruptions of this kind would have to be sustained before they could critically undercut the availability of food. Sustained disruptions could occur, for example, in the case of a widespread outbreak of a communicable disease during which workers may be reluctant to appear at job sites for extended periods. In addition, although it is possible to sustain the flow of some foodstuffs during extended electrical outages, the supply of perishable food products could be significantly reduced in the absence of electricity.

Potential Impacts of Food Sector Hazards

The White House has stated that a successful attack on the nation's agriculture and food system could have "catastrophic health and economic effects." Indeed, regardless of the cause, an adverse food sector event could negatively impact public health, the economy, the public's psychological well-being, and the effectiveness of government. DHS [U.S. Department of Homeland Security] recognizes negative impacts in these four areas as the types of consequences that might result from incidents affecting the nation's critical infrastructures.

Foremost among potential effects are those on public health and safety. Foodborne illness outbreaks currently cause widespread morbidity and mortality. The Centers for Disease Control and Prevention (CDC) estimates that the United States experiences 76 million illnesses, 325,000 hospitalizations, and 5,000 deaths from unintentional food contamination each year. Recent USDA estimates place the annual cost of premature deaths caused by a single common foodborne illness, salmonellosis—an illness resulting from infection with *Salmonella* bacteria—at over $2.1 billion. The current public health burden of unintentional contamination is borne more heavily by vulnerable subpopulations, such as individuals with weakened immune systems. In some cases, sickness from contaminated food results in chronic illness.

Significant public health consequences also are to be anticipated in the event of a well-orchestrated deliberate act of food
contamination. A recent article predicted that over 100,000
Americans—many of them school children—could be poisoned if a single milk truck was contaminated with one gram
of *botulinum* type A toxin. Though some experts questioned the
technical basis for the paper's conclusions and signaled that the
dairy industry had taken appropriate countermeasures to reduce
this threat, a single intentional food contamination event could
sicken thousands.

Economic and Psychological Consequences

Given the size of the food sector, damage to the sector could
undermine the orderly functioning of the economy. The broad
distribution and widespread prevalence of the nation's food processing plants, storage facilities, and retail outlets, along with the
continuous distribution and transportation of food, suggest that
a major contamination event could have a significant disruptive
effect on the national economy. The food industry also accounts
for $60 billion in exports and a positive net balance of trade.
Damage to the nation's food sector could result in the loss of export markets and add to trade deficits.

An incident need not be widespread to cause major harm to
U.S. trade. U.S. beef exports plunged when 119 countries insti-
tuted bans on American beef after "mad cow" disease was found
in a U.S. herd in 2003. Japan, a $1.4 billion annual market for U.S.
beef, partially lifted its ban two years later. Even then, nearly half
of the countries accepting U.S. beef in 2003 had not permitted
the resumption of U.S. beef imports.

Commentators on the subject have observed that an adverse
food sector event could also reduce state and local governments'
ability to maintain order and deliver essential services. A major food contamination event could engender public panic on
a local or mass scale, depending on the affected food product

and population, and media coverage of the incident. Widespread public panic could occur if adulteration of foods resulted in a large number of deaths. An appreciable decline in public confidence in the government could result if a contamination event were linked to a government facility.

Finally, an adverse incident affecting the food sector could undermine public morale and confidence in the nation's institutions. Most Americans currently regard their food as safe. A July 2005 Gallup Poll found that large majorities of respondents were "confident" that food in U.S. grocery stores and restaurants was safe. Because there have been few incidents of large-scale food contamination, it is not clear how the public's perceptions about the safety of food might change in response. The Gilmore Commission reported that a major act of terrorism against the food supply is likely to have "a major psychological impact." It further indicated that the psychological consequences of such an attack were "not well understood."

"In the end, the most probable attack against the food supply is unlikely to create a significant death toll."

The Threat of Bioterrorism to Food Supplies Is Exaggerated

Fred Burton and Scott Stewart

In the following viewpoint, Fred Burton and Scott Stewart claim that bioterrorist attacks on the food supply would not harm or endanger large populations. According to Burton and Stewart, an effective strike on the United States is logistically impossible because of the enormous size of its agriculture industry. Moreover, they insist that producing or obtaining an agent or pathogen with the characteristics needed to cause massive casualties and injuries is difficult. The authors, nonetheless, warn that failed attacks can cause widespread panic and significant economic losses. Burton and Stewart are analysts and senior executives for Stratfor, a global intelligence firm based in Austin, Texas.

As you read, consider the following questions:

1. What obstacles do terrorists face even if they have an effective pathogen, as stated by the authors?

2. Why would a famine resulting from bioterrorism be unlikely, in Burton and Stewart's view?

3. Why are other types of attacks preferred by al Qaeda, in
the authors' opinion?

High food prices have sparked a great deal of unrest over the
past few weeks [in 2008]. Indeed, the skyrocketing cost of
food staples like grain has caused protests involving thousands
of people in places such as South Africa, Egypt and Pakistan.
These protests turned deadly in Haiti and even led to the ouster
of Prime Minister Jacques-Edouard Alexis.

With global food supplies already tight, many people have begun once again to think (and perhaps even worry) about threats
to the U.S. agricultural system and the impact such threats could
have on the U.S.—and global—food supply. In light of this, it is
instructive to examine some of these threats and attempt to place
them in perspective.

A Breakdown of Potential Threats

Since the Sept. 11, 2001, attacks, there have been many reports
issued by various government and civilian sources warning of
the possibility that terrorists could target the U.S. food supply. At
the most basic level, threats to a country's food supply can come
in two general forms: attacks designed to create famine, and attacks designed to directly poison people.

Attacks designed to create famine would entail the use of
some agent intended to kill crops or livestock. Such agents could
include pathogens, insects, or chemicals. The pathogens might
include such livestock diseases as Bovine spongiform encephalopathy (BSE), commonly called mad cow disease, or hoof-and-
mouth disease. Crop diseases such as Ug99 fungus or molds also
pose a threat to supplies.

Attacks designed to poison people could also be further divided into two general forms: those intended to introduce toxins

or pathogens prior to processing and those intended to attack finished food products. Attacks against foodstuffs during agricultural production could include placing an agent on crops in the field or while in transit to a mill or processing center. Attacks against finished foodstuffs would entail covertly placing the toxin or pathogen into the finished food product after processing.

It must be noted that an attack against people could also be conducted for the purposes of creating a mass disruption—such action would not be designed to cause mass casualties, but rather to create fear, unrest and mistrust of the government and food supply, or to promote hoarding. In fact, based on historical examples of incidents involving the contamination of food products, such an attack is far more likely to occur than a serious systematic attack on the food supply.

Attack Constraints

While attacks against the food supply may appear simple in theory, they have occurred infrequently—and for good reason: When one considers the sheer size of the U.S. agricultural sector, conducting a productive assault proves difficult.

As seen by the coca and marijuana eradication efforts by the United States and its partners in Mexico, Central America and the Andes, the logistical effort needed to make any substantial dent in agricultural production is massive. Even the vast resources the United States has dedicated to drug eradication tasks in small countries—overt plane flights spraying untold thousands of gallons of herbicides for decades—have failed to create more than a limited effect on marijuana and coca crops. Obviously, any sort of meaningful chemical attack on U.S. agriculture would have to be so massive that it is simply not logistically feasible.

This is where pathogens—agents that can, at least in theory, be introduced in limited amounts, reproduce and then rapidly spread to infect a far larger area—enter the picture. In order to be effective, however, a pathogen must be one that is easily spread and very deadly and has a long incubation period (in order to ensure it is passed along before the host dies). It is also very helpful to the propagation of a disease if it is difficult to detect and/or difficult to treat. While a pathogen that possesses all of the aforementioned traits could be devastating, finding such an agent is difficult. Few diseases have all the requisite characteristics. Some are very deadly, but act too quickly to be passed, while others are more readily passed but do not have a long incubation period or are not as virulent. Other pathogens, such as the Ug99 wheat fungus, are easy to detect and kill. There is also the problem of mutation, meaning that many pathogens tend to mutate into less virulent actors. It is also important to note that genetically engineering a super bug—one that possesses all the characteristics to make it highly effective—is still much harder in real life than it is on television.

Even if such an effective pathogen is found, someone intending to use it in an attack must isolate the virulent strain, manufacture it in sufficient quantities to be effective, ship it to the place of the planned attack and then distribute it in a manner whereby it is effectively dispersed. The infrastructure required to undertake such an endeavor is both large and expensive. Even in past cases where groups possessed the vast monetary resources to fund biological weapons efforts and amassed the scientific expertise to attempt such a program—Aum Shinrikyo comes to mind—virulent pathogens have proven very difficult to produce and effectively disperse in large quantities.

Another factor making these sorts of attacks difficult to orchestrate is the very nature of farming. For thousands of years, farmers have been battling plant and animal diseases. Most of the pathogens that are mentioned in connection with attacks against agriculture include elements already existing in nature such as hoof-and-mouth disease, H5N1 bird flu or a fungus like Ug99. As a result, farmers and governmental organizations such as the Animal and Plant Health Inspection Service have systems in place to monitor crops and animals for signs of pathogens.

Sorting Actual Risks from Internalized Fears

In his oft-quoted resignation speech, former U.S. Health and Human Services Secretary Tommy G. Thompson helpfully said, "I, for the life of me, cannot understand why the terrorists have not, you know, attacked our food supply because it is so easy to do." Others write breathlessly that "the terrorist threat of deliberate contamination of the U.S. food supply is real". In 2003, the U.S. Food and Drug Administration (FDA) declassified a document in which they "concluded that there is a high likelihood, over the course of a year, that a significant number of people will be affected by an act of food terrorism." Given that these types of statements appear simply to be examples of "fact-free analysis", they do little to help policymakers sort out actual risk from risks that exist only as a reflection of internalized fears. As the terrorism scholar Brian Michael Jenkins writes "the danger arises when speculation becomes the basis for launching costly efforts to prevent 'what ifs'."

G.R. Dalziel, Food Defence Incidents
1950–2008: A Chronology and Analysis
of Incidents Involving the Malicious
Contamination of the Food Supply
Chain, *2009.*

When these pathogens appear, action is taken and diseased crops are treated or eradicated. Animals are treated or culled. Even in past cases where massive eradication and culling efforts occurred—BSE in the United Kingdom, citrus canker in Florida or the many bird flu outbreaks over the past few years—the measures have not crippled or affected the country's agricultural sector or the larger economy.

Creating famine and poisoning the food supply are also difficult, given the sheer quantity of agricultural products grown. Applying some sort of toxin before the raw food is processed is difficult, given the volume produced. In fact, much grain is diverted to uses other than human consumption, as when corn is used to produce ethanol or feed livestock. Therefore, if a truckload of corn is poisoned, it might never funnel into the human food chain. Furthermore, even if a truck of contaminated grain were destined for the food chain, by the time it made its way through the process it would likely be too diluted to have any effect. During the production process, contaminated corn would first have to combine with other grain, sit in a silo, be moved and stored again, ground and finally made into a finished food product such as a loaf of cornbread—an unlikely source of poisoning for the end user. Processing, washing, cooking, pasteurizing and refining may all also serve to further dilute, cleanse or damage the pathogen in the targeted product. At this point, food is also inspected for naturally occurring pathogens and toxins. Such inspections could help spot an intentional contamination.

Besides, even contaminating one truckload of grain would require a large amount of toxin. Producing that much toxin would require a substantial infrastructure—one that would require a great deal of time and money to build. Not to mention the difficulty inherent in transporting and delivering the toxin.

Past Attacks Prove Few and Far Between

Actual attacks against food are very rare. And due to the considerations enumerated above, nearly every food attack we are aware of was an attempt to directly poison people and not cause famine. Furthermore, almost all of these attacks involved processed foods or raw foods packaged for human consumption.

While people are frequently sickened by pathogens in food such as *E. coli* or *salmonella* bacteria, most incidents are not intentional. One of the few known successful attempts at using a biological agent to contaminate food in the United States occurred in 1984 in the small Oregon town of The Dalles. Followers of cult leader Bhagwan Shree Rajneesh, attempting to manipulate a local election, infected salad bars in 10 restaurants with *Salmonella typhimurium*, causing about 751 people to become ill.

A second contamination attempt occurred in October 1996, when 12 laboratory workers at a large medical center in Texas experienced severe gastrointestinal illness after eating muffins and doughnuts left in their break room. Laboratory tests revealed that the pastries had been intentionally infected with *S. dysenteriae*, a pathogen that rarely occurs in the United States. An investigation later determined that the pathogen came from a stock culture kept at the lab.

While many people recall the 1989 Chilean grape scare—when two grapes imported to the United States were injected with cyanide—few recall that the perpetrator in the case made several calls to the U.S. Embassy warning of the contamination and was therefore not seriously attempting to harm people, but rather attempting an action designed to draw attention to social injustice in Chile. The warning calls allowed agricultural inspectors to find the damaged and discolored grapes before they were eaten.

In a lesser-known case that took place in 1978, a dozen children in the Netherlands and West Germany were hospitalized after eating oranges imported from Israel. The Arab Revolutionary Council, a nom de guerre [pseudonym] by the Abu Nidal Organization, deliberately contaminated the fruit with mercury in an attempt to damage the Israeli economy.

Potential Players and the Public Impact

Such attacks could potentially be conducted by a wide array of actors, ranging from a single mentally disturbed individual on one end of the spectrum to sovereign nations on the other end. Cults and domestic or transnational terrorist groups fall somewhere in the middle. The motivation behind these diverse actors could range from monetary extortion or attempts to commit mass murder to acts of war designed to cripple the U.S. economy or the nation's ability to project power.

Of these actors, however, there are very few who possess the ability to conduct attacks that could have a substantial impact on the U.S. food supply. In fact, most of the actors are only capable of contaminating finished food products. While they all have this rudimentary capability, there is also the question of intent.

Documents and manuals found in Afghanistan after the 2001 U.S.-led invasion revealed an al Qaeda interest in conducting chemical and biological attacks, although this interest was not a well-developed program. From a cost-benefit standpoint, it would be much cheaper and easier to use explosives to create disruption than it would be to execute a complicated plot against the food supply. Besides, such a target would not produce the type of spectacular imagery the group enjoys.

While we do not foresee any huge attempt by the Russians or Chinese, and food supply is not a part of al Qaeda's preferred target set, it is possible that a lone wolf or a smaller extremist organization could attempt to conduct such an attack. While any such offensive will likely have limited success, it could have far wider societal repercussions. At the present time, the public has become somewhat accustomed to food scares and recalls over things such as contaminated spinach, ground beef and green onions. Even warnings over lead and other harmful chemicals in food imported from China have caused concern.

However, if even a relatively unsuccessful attack on the food supply were conducted by a terrorist group, it could create significant hysteria—especially if the media sensationalized the event. In such a case, even an ineffective terror plot could result in a tremendous amount of panic and economic loss.

Perhaps the best recent example of this type of disruptive attack is the 2001 anthrax letter attacks. Although the attacks only claimed the lives of five victims, they caused a huge, disproportionate effect on the collective American and world psyche. The public fears that arose from the anthrax attacks were augmented by extensive media discussions about the use of the agent as a weapon. The public sense of unease was further heightened by the fact that the perpetrator was never identified or apprehended. As a result, countless instances surfaced in which irrational panic caused office buildings, apartment buildings, government offices and factories to be evacuated. Previously ignored piles of drywall dust and the powdered sugar residue left by someone who ate a donut at his desk led to suspicions about terrorists, who suddenly seemed to be lurking around every corner. It did not matter, in the midst of the fear, that the place where the "anthrax" was found could have absolutely no symbolic or strategic value to the Islamist militants that most Americans pictured in their minds. The sense of threat and personal vulnerability was pervasive.

In the years since 2001, thousands of hoax anthrax letters have been sent to companies, government offices, schools and politicians in the United States and abroad. Many of these hoaxes have caused psychosomatic responses, resulting in victims being hospitalized, and further economic losses in terms of lost production time, emergency hazmat response costs and laboratory tests.

In the end, the most probable attack against the food supply is unlikely to create a significant death toll, but the panic such an attack may evoke can cause repercussions that are far greater than the death toll itself.

"The U.S. has not been the victim of a large-scale, successful agroterrorism attack. However, there are serious vulnerabilities within our agricultural and food processing systems that must be addressed."

Agroterrorism Poses a Threat to US Agriculture

R. Goodrich Schneider, K.R. Schneider, C.D. Webb, M. Hubbard, and D.L. Archer

In the following viewpoint, R. Goodrich Schneider, K.R. Schneider, C.D. Webb, M. Hubbard, and D.L. Archer insist that the domestic agriculture system is vulnerable to terrorist attacks, or agroterrorism. The potential of agroterrorism to disrupt the nation's agriculture export market can intimidate countries that import agricultural products from the United States and financially harm the industry, claim the authors. Farming, processing plants, and other operations are now centralized and consolidated, the authors purport, which would compound the effects of an agroterrorist event. The authors are based at the University of Florida's Institute of Food and Agricultural Sciences, Food Science and Human Nutrition Department.

R. Goodrich Schneider, K.R. Schneider, C.D. Webb, M. Hubbard, and D.L. Archer, "Agroterrorism in the US: An Overview," *Electronic Data Information Source*, 2009. Copyright © 2009 by IFAS—The University of Florida. All rights reserved. Reproduced by permission.

As you read, consider the following questions:

1. What percent of US farm products were exported in 2008?
2. What other reasons do the authors provide for the need of better security in agricultural operations?
3. In what ways can an actual or perceived agroterrorist event be mitigated, as offered by the authors?

Since the attacks of 9/11, vulnerabilities of the nation's infrastructure have been analyzed and discussed. The United States has identified the protection of national systems and infrastructure, such as the transportation, communication, water supply, and agriculture networks, as priorities to defend against terrorism.

Terrorism is widely defined as the unlawful use of force, violence, or implied harm against persons and property to intimidate or coerce a government, the civilian population, or any element of either, to further political, religious, or ideological aims. Agroterrorism is the deliberate introduction of detrimental agents, biological and otherwise, into the agricultural and food processing system with the intent of causing actual or perceived harm. The broad areas of agriculture that could provide targets in an agroterrorism event are farm animals and livestock, plant crops, and the food processing, distribution, and retailing system.

The term bioterrorism will be widely used in this discussion, and in fact is closely related to agroterrorism. Bioterrorism is defined as the use of biological agents in a deliberate, harmful attack, or terrorism using the weapons of biological warfare such as anthrax, smallpox, or other pathogens. Bioterrorism attacks can be directed not only at agricultural targets, but also at the general public and key domestic infrastructure systems and personnel. The anthrax incidents involving tainted mail that occurred shortly after the 9/11 events can be classified as bioterrorism. In the discussion herein, biological agents can be considered the most probable weapon used to launch an agroterrorism event.

Consequences of a US Agroterrorism Event

Agriculture and the food industry are important to the U.S. economy. The USDA's [US Department of Agriculture] Agricultural Research Service (USDA-ARS) estimates one person in eight works in some part of the agriculture/food sector. Cattle and dairy farmers alone earned over $95 billion a year in meat and milk sales in 2007. Domestically, a significant portion of the U.S. Gross Domestic Product (GDP) is related to agriculture and food production.

Even without agroterrorism, livestock and crop diseases cost the U.S. economy billions of dollars annually. These are the baseline losses to which the financial impact of an actual agroterrorism event would be added.

If an agroterrorism event occurred in the U.S., the potential for disruption of our export market would be immense. International trade is crucial, as it provides a market for a major part of our crop production, and a growing share of meat output. Overall, 12.7% of the U.S. GDP was due to international trade in 2008. For comparison, close to 30% of U.S. farm products were exported in 2008, while nonagricultural exports were about 12% of the GDP. Proportionately, the U.S. agriculture industries rely on export markets more heavily than other sectors of U.S. industry. An agroterrorism event that instigated fear or even uncertainty in our international customers could be financially devastating to U.S. agricultural interests.

Vulnerability of the US Agriculture System

Various factors lead to the heightened state of vulnerability of the U.S. to an agroterrorism event. As previously discussed, agriculture, food processing and food retailing contribute significantly to the U.S. economy, despite the perception of the ceaseless encroachment of urban growth into rural areas. As urban growth has occurred, agricultural operations, including farms, packinghouses, and processing plants have become larger, more centralized, and more intensive. It is this type of industrial concentration that perhaps increases the vulnerability of the U.S. agriculture system; as almost all agricultural sectors consolidate, their overall size generally increases. Thus, the impact of a targeted agroterrorism event affecting just one entity could still have a serious, adverse impact. For example, foot-and-mouth disease (FMD) confined to a very small geographically distinct herd is a vastly different situation than FMD occurring through intentional spread of the disease in a large cattle operation. Although large operations typically have greater economies-of-scale, they also lead to these types of vulnerabilities.

There are other reasons to be aware of the need to better security in agricultural operations. It is difficult and expensive to secure large areas of farm land with fences, gates and monitoring devices. Yet, it is incumbent upon producers to provide security in these areas. Packinghouses and processing plants are more easily controlled from a physical perimeter standpoint, but conversely have more personnel that need to be screened and then trained in specifics of plant security. More and more auditors focus on specific areas where their clients can improve their procedures and practices. Defense against terrorism must become ingrained in the normal operations of all agricultural operations before the U.S. can expect an improvement in the current state of readiness against an attack.

The Bioterrorism Act of 2002

The events of 9/11 reinforced the need to enhance the security of the United States. One broad area of vulnerability, as discussed, is the area of agriculture and specifically food production. The term food security, which traditionally meant the stability and supply of sufficient food for a given population, suddenly took

Confidence of Food Safety Among US Residents

4,260 members of the public were asked whether they were confident or not confident that the food supply is safe, and whether they were confident or not confident that the food supply is safe against terrorism.

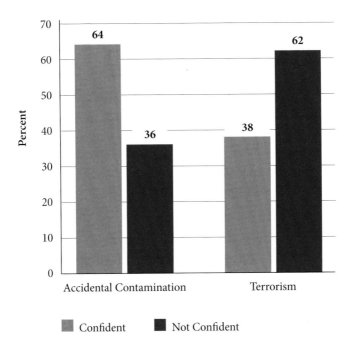

TAKEN FROM: Thomas F. Stinson, Jean Kinsey, Dennis Degeneffe, and Koel Ghosh, "Defending America's Food Supply Against Terrorism: Who Is Responsible? Who Should Pay?," *Choices*, First Quarter, vol. 22, no. 1, 2007.

on a different meaning. On June 12, 2002, the Public Health Security and Bioterrorism Preparedness and Response Act of 2002 (the Act) was signed into law by the U.S. Congress. The FDA [Food and Drug Administration] is responsible for developing and implementing regulations on the following major provisions of the Act: Registration of Food Facilities, Prior Notice of

Imported Food, Establishment and Maintenance of Records, and Administrative Detention. The definition of food used in these regulations includes food and beverages for human and animal consumption, including dietary supplements, infant formula, and food additives. It does not, however, cover food products such as meat and poultry that are regulated by the USDA-FSIS [Food Safety and Inspection Service]. The Act was designed to improve the ability of the U.S. to prevent, prepare for, and respond to bioterrorism and other public health emergencies.

Prevention, Detection, and Mitigation

Ideally, terrorism aimed at the food supply would be 100% preventable. In the aftermath of 9/11, many resources were shifted from food safety to food biosecurity, with the intent to try to install sufficient deterrents that would lead to an improved condition of readiness within the agriculture and food sector. State and federal agencies, along with trade organizations and third-party auditors, developed better and more thorough auditing tools and checklists that focused on security aspects for processing plants, their products and their personnel.

However, experience with naturally occurring outbreaks of foodborne disease has demonstrated that no existing preventive system is 100% effective. To some degree, improved speed of detection of a bioterrorism event can help minimize impact of a particular event. After 9/11, agencies increased their inspection and analytical capabilities in response to increased needs to respond quickly to a bioterrorism threat. The anthrax incidents that occurred after 9/11, although not specifically agroterrorism, highlighted to the authorities the need for a networked system of laboratories with pathogen and toxin detection capabilities.

Mitigation is one means of dealing with an actual or threatened agroterrorism event. The FDA, through the Bioterrorism Act of 2002, is requiring all food plants to register with the agency. They are also requiring prior notice for imported food shipments, as well as better record-keeping on the part of food processors and handlers. Should prevention fail, public safety falls to mitigation and containment strategies. One of the reasons the FDA is requesting this information is to enhance traceability of food products and the efficacy of product recalls. Recalls involve removing product from the commerce stream after they have left the distributor. Product may be in-transit, at the retail level, or even in the individual consumer's home. Retrieving the potentially contaminated product before it can be consumed is an effective way to limit the public health impact of contaminated food. Most biosecurity audits within food processing, handling, and retailing facilities now identify product recalls, and the ability to quickly and effectively execute them, as an important approach to their overall anti-terrorism strategy.

The U.S. has not been the victim of a large-scale, successful agroterrorism attack. However, there are serious vulnerabilities within our agricultural and food processing systems that must be addressed. Through an iterative process of risk assessment, risk control, and verification of implemented deterrents, all pertinent agricultural interests, regulators, scientists, and public health officials can improve the defensive position of this key industry and strive to reduce the threat of agroterrorism as much as possible.

| "The fear of agroterrorism has been blown out of all proportion."

The Threat of Agroterrorism to US Agriculture Is Exaggerated

Mary Zanoni, interviewed by Chuck Jolley

In the following viewpoint, Mary Zanoni argues that fears of agroterrorism, or terrorist strikes on farming and livestock operations, are overblown. She points out that current regulatory efforts and requirements are unnecessary and do not protect farmers, cattle raisers, and growers. Food production centers are not attractive targets to terrorist groups, Zanoni adds. If the federal government wants to effectively aid US agriculture, she concludes, it must address the crisis of resources the industry faces. Chuck Jolley is a Kansas-based writer covering the agriculture industry. Zanoni is executive director of Farm for Life, an advocacy group for local and sustainable agriculture.

As you read, consider the following questions:

1. What is "hay tracking," as described by the author?
2. What is the only way a hayfield can be protected from microbes released by terrorists, in Zanoni's view?

3. If agroterrorism is a real threat, what is the best assurance against it, as offered by Zanoni?

Chuck Jolley: You've said, "Real food security comes from rais-ing food yourself or buying from a local farmer you actually know. The USDA [US Department of Agriculture] plan will only stifle local sources of production through over-regulation and un-manageable costs." Fair enough, but one of the growing concerns about the safety of our food supply is the threat of agro-terrorism. It could devastate all farming operations regardless of size. How would you propose to combat that possibility?

Mary Zanoni: The fear of "agro-terrorism" has been blown out of all proportion. In this respect, it's noteworthy that pundits of all stripes have emphasized the recent tendency of our own Federal government to create and exploit "fear" among the citizens, for the apparent benefit of those who occupy positions of power.

One example of an overblown fear of "agro-terrorism" is the FDA's [Food Drug Administration] "hay tracking" requirements going into effect this year. These require people who sell hay to keep records of what fields which hay comes from, all people who worked on harvesting or transporting the hay, interim stor-age of the hay, and identity and location of the buyer of the hay. The only "saving grace" of this ridiculous regulation is that paper records are sufficient and apparently the hay seller does not have to submit the records to any government agency, but rather, is simply required to keep the records for a period of time in case the government comes around asking for them. Still, tech-related recordkeeping companies have come forward pushing products that will computerize these records for hay sellers. Undoubtedly the requirements will increase hay prices for at least some buyers.

But we get literally nothing for all the added hassle and ex-pense. If a criminal wanted to sprinkle some poison or microbe on a hayfield, the only way to prevent it would be to post sev-eral armed guards at every hayfield 24/7/365. That's crazy and impossible, so instead the FDA promulgates the ridiculous hay rules, which do nothing to make anyone safer.

As far as "terrorism" is concerned, isn't it obvious that terrorists like to go after airplanes and crowded urban locations? Don't you think "agro-terrorism" is pretty far down on the terrorists' "to-do" list? Wouldn't you feel safer if the government stopped wasting money and time on NAIS [the National Animal Identification System] and hay rules, and instead directed those resources toward helping to locate all those missing Soviet nuclear materials, or developing better airport bomb-detection equipment?

Further, even assuming any realistic threat of "agro-terrorism," the best insurance against it would be a diverse, geographically dispersed system of food production. Would it be harder for a "terrorist" to hit a single 100,000-bird broiler operation, or 5,000 separate 20-bird backyard flocks? The answer is obvious and industrial agriculture simply can't deny the fact that more and more concentration of production makes our food supply more and more vulnerable to either accidental or deliberate disruption.

On the other hand, even if someone or something destroys one of the 5,000 private small flocks, you still have 4,999 other citizens with a reliable at-home source of meat and eggs. So having more small-scale raising of chickens, pigs, cattle, sheep, and goats is, in fact, the way to combat the threat of "agro-terrorism," if indeed there is such a threat.

Alternative Plans

OK, accepting you're firmly against NAIS as proposed but acknowledging something that can effectively protect animal health and food security is important, what alternative plan would you suggest?

Anything that would encourage more small-scale agriculture would help protect animal health and food security. In addition, if the government sincerely wants to address the most crucial present problems facing American agriculture and the American food supply, the following three projects could greatly benefit from the funds now being squandered on NAIS:

A. Several crucial agricultural regions of the U.S. have been plagued by a multi-year drought. This is a predictable effect of global warming and a serious long-term threat to our crop and animal production. We deserve a government that admits the obvious existence of global warming and starts to design some programs for mitigating its effects on agriculture.

B. Over the coming decades fossil fuels will become scarcer. Bio-fuels such as ethanol will not be a "magic bullet" for this problem because it has been demonstrated that production of ethanol uses as much fuel as it creates. A responsible government would initiate real programs to wean our society and economy away from dependence on disappearing fossil fuels, and not lull us into complacency by overemphasis on bio-fuels.

C. Many rural areas suffer a real shortage of large-animal veterinarians. The government needs to address this shortage through recruiting and the provision of scholarships for people who will agree to serve as practicing large-animal vets for a period of years after graduation. The government should also develop programs for training and certifying large-animal veterinary assistants, who could be given responsibilities similar to those exercised by physicians' assistants in human medicine.

Periodical and Internet Sources Bibliography

The following articles have been selected to supplement the diverse views presented in this chapter.

Sharon Begley	"Weaponized Hamburgers?," *Newsweek*, July 16, 2007.
Hilton Collins	"How Fighting Terrorism Indirectly Affected the Food Supply," *Emergency Management*, January 27, 2012.
Simon Cooper	"North Korea's Biochemical Threat," *Popular Mechanics*, October 1, 2009.
Mark D'Agostino and Greg Martin	"The Bioscience Revolution and the Biological Weapons Threat: Levers and Interventions," *Globalization and Health*, vol. 5, 2009.
H. Patricia Hines	"Biological Weapons: Bargaining With the Devil," *Truthout*, August 18, 2011.
Eric Lipton and Scott Shane	"Anthrax Case Renews Questions on Bioterror," *New York Times*, August 3, 2008.
Matthew Padilla	"Preparing for the Unknown: The Threat of Agroterrorism," *Sustainable Law Development and Policy*, Fall 2008.
Suhda Raman	"The Emerging Biological Weapons Threat and Proliferation," *CBW Magazine*, January 2009.
Eric Savitz	"Agroterrorism: Managing Risk in The Food Supply Chain," *Forbes*, April 19, 2011.
Jeffrey D. Simon	"Why the Bioterrorism Skeptics Are Wrong," *Journal of Bioterrorism and Biodefense*, October 20, 2011.
Marcus Stern	"Experts Divided Over Risk of Bioterrorist Attack," *ProPublica*, December 5, 2008.

OPPOSING
VIEWPOINTS®
SERIES

CHAPTER 2

What Are the Issues Associated with Biodefense Research?

Chapter Preface

In late 2011, virologist Ron Fouchier and a team of scientists in the Netherlands announced they created "probably one of the most dangerous viruses you can make." It is a deadly strain of avian influenza, H5N1, but genetically modified to spread easily in humans. To investigate how H5N1 can become more virulent, the researchers produced mutations that enabled it to be transmitted airborne in mammals; ferrets were infected just from being in cages near each another. If set loose, some claim, the virus could spark a pandemic and kill hundreds of millions worldwide, as half of those infected may die. "I can't think of another pathogenic organism that is as scary as this one," claims Paul Keim, a microbial geneticist. "I don't think anthrax is scary at all compared to this."

In fact, numerous experts warn that information from Fouchier's research on H5N1 could be used by terrorists to launch a biological attack of unprecedented proportions. "[I]t would have characteristics of an ultimate biological weapon unknown even in science fiction," argues D.A. Henderson, a smallpox researcher at the University of Pittsburgh's Center for Biosecurity. "We should not publish a blueprint for constructing such an organism." The National Science Advisory Board for Biosecurity (NSABB), a federal agency, requested that specific details from Fouchier's research and a similar one at University of Wisconsin-Madison be withheld in the science journals *Nature* and *Science*, which postponed publication of the studies.

Yet others in the scientific community are concerned that such restrictions on research may not prevent bioterrorist attacks. "Censoring scientific data for publication will not stop rogue individuals or nations from developing a deadly and highly transmissible form of H5N1," asserts Kwok-yung Yuen, chair of infectious disease at the University of Hong Kong's Department of Microbiology. In addition, Fouchier himself persists that the

NSABB's request to withhold his findings hinders health organizations and facilities from preparing for an influenza outbreak. "NSABB gives very little credit to the public health benefits, while the entire influenza community is crying just how important that is. For them, the balance between risk and benefit is very different than for NSABB," he states.

In the following chapter, authors debate issues facing bioterrorism research such as safety and adequate oversight.

| *"The conduct and management of pathogen research have evolved in response to concerns about safety and, more recently, security."*

Biodefense Research Is Safe

Committee on Special Immunizations Program for Laboratory Personnel Engaged in Research on Countermeasures for Select Agents

In the following viewpoint, the Committee on Special Immunizations Program for Laboratory Personnel Engaged in Research on Countermeasures for Select Agents claims that biodefense research is guided by practice and procedure frameworks that minimize risk, ensuring both laboratory and national security. For instance, the committee maintains that facilities with high or maximum biological containment are specialized for research on the most dangerous pathogens, and researchers must adhere to strict procedures. Also, pathogens are thoroughly categorized based on several criteria, the committee explains, including the potential to cause harm, availability of treatments, and ease of production and dissemination. The committee is part of the National Research Council, providing studies and investigations for the US National Academies.

Committee on Special Immunizations Program for Laboratory Personnel Engaged in Research on Countermeasures for Select Agents, *Protecting the Frontline in Biodefense Research: The Special Immunizations Program*, 2011, pp. 9–13. Washington, DC: US National Academies. Copyright © 2011 by the US National Academies. All rights reserved. Reproduced by permission.

As you read, consider the following questions:

1. According to the committee, how are BSL-4 laboratories described?
2. How is access to pathogens restricted, as explained by the committee?
3. How does the committee characterize the risk to laboratory workers of accidental exposure to pathogens and toxins?

For more than 200 years, from the earliest discoveries of such luminaries as Edward Jenner, Robert Koch, and Louis Pasteur[1] to the present day, scientists have conducted research on microorganisms and other pathogens that cause infectious diseases. Their research has produced vaccines and therapies that have greatly decreased the risks posed by infectious diseases. As a National Research Council committee noted in 2009, "it is not an exaggeration to attribute increased human lifespan and better human health to the research of legions of microbiologists and other biomedical researchers on the biology of bacteria and viruses and the toxins they produce". Research on microorganisms improves our ability to prevent infectious disease outbreaks, to treat them more effectively when they occur, and to detect the pathogens and toxins more rapidly both in patients and in the environment.

Shortly after the September 11, 2001, attacks, the United States received a new impetus to support and conduct pathogen research when a second set of attacks occurred, this time involving the bacterium *Bacillus anthracis*, the etiologic agent of the disease anthrax. Since then, the nation's capacity to conduct pathogen research has expanded substantially. According to a recent analysis of the biodefense budget, U.S. government civilian biodefense funding increased from $633.4 million in FY [fiscal year] 2001 to a requested $6.5 billion in FY 2011, which brought the U.S. government investment during FY 2001–2011 to a total of $61.9 billion. In FY 2011, $4.7 billion of the requested $6.5 billion (over 70%) is for HHS [Health and Human Services], and 37% of this amount ($1.75 billion) is for the National Institutes of Health (NIH) to support research related to biodefense.

An important outcome of the funding amplification has been an expansion of the research infrastructure. The number of biological safety level (BSL) 4 laboratories—which are used for research on the most dangerous pathogens, those that pose the highest risk of disease and for which no vaccine or therapy is available—increased from two before 1990 to at least seven in 2009, with a projected expansion to at least thirteen. Such laboratories are no longer limited to the federal government but now include facilities in academic institutions, state and local public health departments, and the private sector. The number of the much more numerous BSL-3 laboratories is unknown, but they also underwent rapid expansion during that period. Those increases in pathogen research laboratory capacity were made possible largely by the substantial influx of federal support already noted. For example, since 2003, the National Institute of Allergy and Infectious Diseases (NIAID) has supported the development of eleven Regional Centers of Excellence for Biodefense and Emerging Infectious Diseases (RCEs) and twelve Regional Biocontainment Laboratories (RBLs). Each RCE comprises a consortium of universities and research institutions that serve a specific geographic region. In the RCE program alone, there are nearly 500 principal investigators, mostly new to biodefense, in almost 300 participating institutions.

Categorization of Pathogens and Management of Pathogen Research

The conduct and management of pathogen research have evolved in response to concerns about safety and, more recently, security. This evolution has produced a number of practice and procedure frameworks that incorporate consideration of the relative risks of research on hazardous infectious microorganisms due to their biological properties and their potential as biological weapons (bioweapons).

Over the last twenty-five years, best practices have been designed, articulated, and accepted to reduce the likelihood that research with hazardous pathogens will cause harm either to laboratory workers or to the public or the environment because of accidents or accidental releases. HHS published the first edition of its *Biosafety in Microbiological and Biomedical Laboratories (BMBL)* in 1984, and the fifth edition was issued in 2007 and revised in December 2009. Although not codified in formal regulations, the *BMBL* guidelines are widely used performance-based criteria for how modern pathogen research laboratories are expected to operate. *BMBL* from its inception has constituted a set of guidelines for laboratory safety in the academic, government, and public health communities. *BMBL* categorizes infectious pathogens and laboratory activities into four biosafety levels (BSL-1 through BSL-4) and establishes safety guidelines for each level on the basis of risk:

- BSL-1 laboratories are designed for work with pathogens and toxins that do not consistently cause disease in healthy human adults.

- BSL-2 laboratories are designed for work with pathogens and toxins that can be spread by puncture, absorption through mucus membranes, or ingestion.

- BSL-3 laboratories are designed for work with pathogens and toxins that are capable of aerosol transmission and that may cause serious or lethal infection.

- BSL-4 laboratories are designed for work with pathogens and toxins that pose a high risk of life-threatening disease, that are capable of aerosol transmission, and for which there is generally no available therapy or vaccine.

BSL-3 and BSL-4 laboratories are considered to afford "high" and "maximum" biological containment (biocontainment), respectively, for research on the most dangerous pathogens. They

Biodefense Research at the National Institute of Allergy and Infectious Diseases

NIAID's biodefense research runs the entire spectrum from basic research to the development of new diagnostics, drugs, and vaccines. The research program includes target identification, preclinical development, and clinical evaluation of experimental products. Research resources, such as new laboratories and genomics information, are also essential. The Institute's initiatives involve NIAID scientists, academia, and industry....

Basic research includes pathogen biology—research into the basic microbiology and pathogenesis of emerging infectious diseases and the microorganisms and toxins that may be used as agents of bioterrorism. Related activities include microbial genomic sequencing and proteomics.

Research also focuses on host response to these organisms and toxins. To develop potent, safe, and effective vaccines; accurate diagnostics; and immunotherapeutics, it is critical to improve our understanding of the complex parameters of innate and adaptive immunity. Because most potential bioterror agents would infect via the respiratory or oral routes, emphasis is also placed on studies of mucosal immunity at these sites. Crosscutting, multidisciplinary research will facilitate translation of this basic knowledge into vaccines, therapies, and diagnostic methods focused on bioterrorist agents. In addition, new discoveries of immunologic principles or applications will help ensure a robust pipeline of improved or novel products for biodefense, emerging infectious diseases, and many other diseases.

National Institute of Allergy and Infectious Diseases, August 10, 2010. www.niaid.gov.

require specialized expertise to design, construct, commission, operate, and maintain, and workers in these laboratories must follow stringent safety procedures and use specialized safety equipment. High- and maximum-containment laboratories may also be necessary for some diagnostic and analytic services.

The *BMBL* guidelines are not regulations, but research on many pathogens is subject to regulatory oversight via other programs, such as the HHS-USDA [US Department of Agriculture] Select Agent program. The program was created in 1996 by the Antiterrorism and Effective Death Penalty Act (Public Law 104-132), which was passed amid rising concerns about terrorism after a number of terrorist acts, including the Oklahoma City bombing. Before 2001, the statute governed primarily the transfer of biological pathogens and toxins between research laboratories. The act directed the secretary of HHS and the secretary of USDA to regulate the transport of biological agents that have the potential to pose severe threats to public, animal, or plant health and safety through their use in bioterrorism. The HHS secretary delegated that authority to the Centers for Disease Control and Prevention (CDC) and the USDA secretary to the Animal and Plant Health Inspection Service (APHIS). To ensure that the pathogens and toxins were transferred only between responsible parties, CDC and APHIS required that laboratories that transfer Select Agents be registered and that transfers be reported to CDC and APHIS and conducted under a permitting system.

Expansion of Regulations for Select Agents

After the anthrax attacks of 2001, the regulations governing Select Agents were greatly expanded under the Public Health Security and Bioterrorism Preparedness and Response Act of 2002 into a rigorous and formal oversight system to ensure that persons seeking to possess, use, or transfer Select Agents or Toxins have a lawful purpose. Among its requirements, the law:

- Requires all facilities possessing Select Agents to register with the secretary of HHS or USDA, not just facilities sending or receiving Select Agents. Registration is for three years, and facilities must demonstrate that they meet the requirements delineated in *BMBL* for working with particular Select Agents. Such requirements include having proper laboratory and personal protective equipment, precautionary signs, monodirectional and high-efficiency particulate air (HEPA) filtered ventilation, controlled access, and biosafety operations manuals. Facilities must describe the laboratory procedures that will be used, provide a floor plan of the laboratory where Select Agents will be handled and stored, and describe how access will be limited to authorized personnel. And facilities must describe the objectives of the work that requires use of Select Agents. Each facility must identify a responsible facility official who is authorized to transfer and receive Select Agents on behalf of the facility.

- Restricts access to pathogens and toxins by persons who do not have a legitimate need and who are considered by federal law-enforcement and intelligence officials to pose a risk.

- Requires transfer registrations to include information regarding the characterization of pathogens and toxins to facilitate their identification, including their source.

- Requires the creation of a national database with information on all facilities and persons that possess, use, or transfer Select Agents.

- Directs the secretaries of HHS and USDA to review and publish the Select Agents list biennially, making revisions as appropriate to protect the public.

- Requires the secretaries of HHS and USDA to impose more detailed and different levels of security for different Select Agents on the basis of their assessed level of threat to the public.

The regulations are applicable to all federal, public, and private research institutions and individuals associated with the institutions that possess, handle, store, and conduct research activities and programs that use Select Agents and Toxins. The Select Agents list is maintained by CDC for human pathogens and toxins and by APHIS for plant and animal pathogens. The list, first introduced in 1997, has grown from forty-two pathogens and toxins to the current eighty-two, forty pathogens are HHS-only agents, thirty-two are USDA-only agents (twenty-four animal pathogens and eight plant pathogens), and ten are zoonotic pathogens that overlap both HHS and USDA.

Criteria of Pathogens Conferred as Select Agents

The criteria for including a particular pathogen or toxin on the Select Agents list address threats to public, animal, and plant health and safety but go further to include more security-oriented considerations. Historically, pathogens that had been previously weaponized by the United States or other countries have been considered to pose the greatest risks, including the ability to incapacitate affected people or cause highly lethal infections in a short period, lack of availability of preventive or therapeutic measures, ease of production, stability as an aerosol, and capability of being dispersed as small particles. The following considerations have generally been used as the basis for conferring Select Agent status on particular microorganisms. Some of them deal with health risks, others with potency or effectiveness as potential biological weapon (bioweapons):

- Virulence, pathogenicity, or toxicity of the microorganism; its potential to cause death or serious disease.

- Availability of treatments, such as vaccines or drugs, to control the consequences of a release or epidemic.

- Transmissibility of the microorganism; its potential to cause an uncontrolled epidemic.

- Ease of preparing the microorganism in sufficient quantity and stability for use as a biological terrorism (bioterrorism) agent, for example, the ability to prepare large quantities of stable microbial spores.
- Ease of disseminating the microorganism in a bioterrorism event to cause mass casualties, for example, by aerosolization.
- Public perception of the microorganism; its potential to cause societal disruption by mass panic.
- Known research and development efforts on the microorganism by national bioweapons programs.

NIAID has also developed a classification of pathogens using a category A, B, and C system. The system is used to set research priorities and uses different criteria for classification. The criteria stress ease of dissemination, associated mortality after infection, potential for public health impact and social disruption, and required special action for public health preparedness. A larger universe of pathogens is included in the NIH assessment, and some pathogens on the NIH list are not captured on the Select Agents list.

It should be clear from the foregoing discussion that research with hazardous pathogens and toxins is associated with a risk of accidental exposure. Many of the laboratory workers, technicians, and others who are exposed to these pathogens and toxins are part of the broad military and public health enterprise to develop medical countermeasures against potential biological threat (biothreat) agents and emerging infectious diseases. However, the current view in the United States is that these risks are part of a necessary investment to protect public health, agriculture, and national security. In addition, risks to laboratory workers are mitigated by laboratory best practices, equipment, facilities, and in some cases the availability of additional protections in the form of vaccines, antibiotics, antiviral drugs, and antibodies.

Note

1. Edward Jenner is well known for his investigations on the use of cowpox vaccination to protect against smallpox, and Robert Koch formulated the criteria in "Koch's postulates" to establish whether a specific microorganism causes a specific disease and isolated *Bacillus anthracis*, among other discoveries. Louis Pasteur discovered that the growth of microorganisms causes fermentation and investigated microbial theories of disease; he did early work on the development of rabies and anthrax vaccines.

> *"The risk is increasing with the expansion [of biodefense research], and is greatest at new facilities lacking experience with standard safety protocols."*

Biodefense Research Is Unsafe

Kenneth King

In the following viewpoint excerpted from his book, Germs Gone Wild: How the Unchecked Development of Domestic Biodefense Threatens America, *Kenneth King contends that biodefense research poses a threat to the nation's security. Hundreds of these facilities contain the most dangerous known pathogens—many of which have no cures or treatments—increasing access to toxins and risks of accidental outbreaks, King argues. In addition, the anti-terrorist fixation on biodefense diverts resources from other projects important to public health, he says, and leads to the rapid proliferation of these facilities. King is author of* Germs Gone Wild *and former English professor at Western Kentucky University.*

As you read, consider the following questions:

1. How does King describe Biosafety Level Four labs?
2. What are the risks of the growing numbers of biodefense

Kenneth King, "Chapter One: A Biodefense Juggernaut," *Germs Gone Wild: How the Unchecked Development of Domestic Biodefense Threatens America*. New York: Pegasus Books, 2010, pp. 1–4, 8–14. Copyright © 2012 by Pegasus Books. All rights reserved. Reproduced by permission.

research facilities at universities, in King's view?

3. In what context does the author place biodefense research in the history of the United States?

On April 23, 2007, America's "war on terror" sent emissaries to a rural pasture in south central Kentucky. They arrived by military helicopter and a van and car convoy escorted by sheriff's deputies and state police. The convoy passed a cluster of protesters holding signs such as "Hal No! No Bio-Lab!" and "The Chamber of Commerce Is Not the Community."

Nearly six thousand people from this heavily Republican, largely rural district had signed petitions asking the Department of Homeland Security (DHS) *not* to bring the country's second biggest biodefense facility to this particular plot of land, despite the fact that their congressman, county judge, mayor, city council, fiscal court, Chamber of Commerce, and local newspaper had spoken on their behalf and told DHS what a perfect spot this would be for a $550 million bio-bonanza.

Like people in other rural communities alarmed by NBAF (the National Bio and Agro-Defense Facility), they had been told by the local "influentsia" that they were backward and ignorant for worrying about this Homeland Security-controlled facility and its Pandoric tinkerings with a yet-to-be-specified list of incurable pathogens. It would be "as safe as going to Wal-Mart," their congressman said. It would be "state of the art." It would be a "quantum leap."

Despite those exhortations, 2,800 people had signed petitions opposing the facility during two weeks in March 2006. Another 2,000 people had signed during the next two months. The rest had trickled in afterward, without any major efforts to sustain the initial drive. In the meantime, opponents had held two major rallies, established a Web site with Fact Sheets and a video, appeared on radio and television, and written a slew of letters and op-eds to local and state newspapers.

Now, over a hundred of them had gathered, on short notice, to confront the Homeland Security inspectors as they tried to slip quietly into the county and out. Channel 36, a Lexington television station, filmed the protesters, the stone-faced passage of the official convoy, and the setdown of the military chopper. After the convoy had passed, the protesters followed them part of the way back, stopping at the boundary of the proposed lab site.

For thirty minutes or so, as the inspectors assessed the bio-tech potential of Kentucky pasture, the protesters chanted slogans: "No Bio Lab!" "No Fort Detrick!" "No Plum Island!" Some people shouted more spontaneous comments: "Where's Hal Rogers?" (Rogers was the U.S. Representative chiefly responsible for DHS's interest in Kentucky). "Look at this beautiful country! You ought to be ashamed of yourselves!" "This is our home! You go back to yours!" A large state trooper loomed near the boundary line, screening the protesters from the entourage of inspectors and inspector-handlers. That evening, Channel 36 spliced together a two-minute newscast. Prominent in the newscast was the military helicopter, dropping out of the sky like a predatory bird, like the shock troops for an armed invasion. . . .

Few would have considered Pulaski County a central battleground in the war on terror, but former Homeland Security Director [Tom] Ridge said DHS funded the National Institute for Home*town* Security under the "unique notion that the homeland is not secure until the hometown is secure." Science Applications International Corporation [SAIC], a leading biodefense contractor, explained its opening of operations in the county not as a subtle form of influence-peddling, but as a spiritual quest to soak up the Hal Rogers zeitgeist: "Being close to leadership helps us understand trends in government." Apparently standard Washington lobbyist come-ons weren't intimate enough for SAIC.

Once the congressman had established his Homeland Security beachheads, however, he wanted more. And so he went after NBAF, a proposed human, animal, and zoonotic disease supercenter surpassed in size only by the new "biodefense campus" at Fort Detrick in Maryland. The new NBAF will be controlled by DHS, and like Detrick, will include Biosafety Level Four (BSL-4) labs—studying diseases for which no vaccine or cure exists—as a major component [The Kentucky site was ultimately not chosen for the biodefense facility]. . . .

A Mindless Proliferation of Deadly Pathogens

DHS's NBAF project is part of a huge explosion in biodefense funding and construction following the anthrax letter attacks of 2001. That event has led to a seven-fold increase in biodefense funding, a twelvefold increase in BSL-4 lab space, and a mushrooming of BSL-3 labs so vast no one in the country knows how many are actually out there. The only tracking of numbers is through the CDC [Centers for Disease Control and Prevention] and USDA [US Department of Agriculture] "Select Agent" programs—labs working with pathogens on the CDC's select agent list are required to register—and there were 1,356 of those BSL-3 labs in October 2007.

BSL-4 labs study the world's deadliest diseases, things like Ebola and the Marburg virus for which no cure or effective treatment currently exists. Researchers work out of pressurized space suits with their own oxygen supply, to avoid breathing or otherwise coming into contact with death-penalty pathogens. They hope to avoid needle pricks or tears in their suits: otherwise they might become casualties of their own work, or, even worse, carry disease out of the fortress-like labs into the community at large—something that happened with high-containment SARS [severe acute respiratory syndrome] labs in Asia in 2003. Until the 1990s the only BSL-4 facilities in the US were USAMRIID [US Army Medical Research Institute of Infectious Diseases] at Fort Detrick and the CDC in Atlanta. By 2000 there were four operational BSL-4 labs. Counting those already constructed and others on the books, there will soon be fifteen.

BSL-3 labs study diseases that are deadly enough, but for which there is some possibility of vaccination or treatment. They feature the same safety protocols as BSL-4 labs except for the space suits. Again, no one knows how many BSL-3 labs are out there, except that the number exceeds 1,356. In February 2008, there were only eight times that many Starbucks in the country, and perhaps the Hazelnut Latte isn't the appropriate business model for biowarfare agents. (Starbucks closed 600 stores a few months later; America's biodefense program has gone the other direction.) Work with anthrax requires only a BSL-2 rating, or BSL-3 if there is a chance of the anthrax becoming aerosolized: there is some sort of vaccine, and the disease can be successfully treated if the right antibiotics are started soon after exposure. This assumes early symptoms aren't confused with the flu and other respiratory ailments. Given the proliferation of biodefense research, probably more U.S. labs have access to anthrax now than at any time in our history (more than 350, according to a 2004 *San Francisco Chronicle* article). The same is true of other biowarfare agents, and that ought to trouble us, given that DNA testing long ago narrowed the source of the 2001 anthrax to four or five existing biodefense facilities.

Distorting the Focus and Research of Public Health Agencies

The new fixation on biodefense has distorted the focus and research of such traditional public health agencies as the Centers for Disease Control and the National Institutes of Health [NIH], turning them into biodefense apologists and infusing them with cultural norms more traditionally associated with defense and intelligence agencies. Though there are certainly scientists eager to capitalize on the new funding cornucopia, others see the new focus as harmful and self-defeating. In 2005, 758 of the 1,143 scientists receiving NIH funding for microbiology research signed an open letter stating that "The diversion of research funds from projects of public-health importance to projects of high bio-

Problems of an Unforeseen Nature

Other dangers arise via routine operations, neither accidents nor intended malice, that turn up problems of an unforeseen nature. For example, an effort to catalog select agent culture collections in Department of Defense facilities in 2008 led to unanticipated and astonishing problems. After months of investigation, USAMRIID reported in June 2009 that no fewer than 9,202 uncataloged microbial culture vials had been found in 335 freezers and refrigerators at the laboratory. Since the official database had listed 66,000 items, the "missing" increment represented about 13 percent of the total. There were two lessons from this incident. First, a CDC investigation of USAMRIID in September 2008 did not discover the problem of unlisted samples. Second, neither USAMRIID nor other U.S. Army biodefense laboratories had previously made complete inventories despite legislation in force since 2002 requiring them to do so.

Milton Leitenberg, Benjamin H. Friedman, Jim Harper, and Christopher A. Preble, eds., Terrorizing Ourselves: Why US Counterterrorism Policy Is Failing and How to Fix It. *Washington, DC: Cato Institute, 2010.*

defense relevance but low public-health importance represents a misdirection of NIH priorities and a crisis for NIH-supported microbiological research."

In October 2007, the Oversight and Investigations subcommittee of the House Energy and Commerce committee conducted a hearing titled "Germs, Viruses, and Secrets: The Silent

Proliferation of Bio-Laboratories in the United States." The hearing's star witness was Dr. Keith Rhodes, Chief Technologist of the Government Accountability Office, who had been investigating the proliferation for two different congressional subcommittees. Also invited were representatives from the CDC, NIH, watchdog groups, and biodefense think tanks, and the president of Texas A&M University, where all "select agent" research had just been suspended by the CDC. Chairman Bart Stupak pointedly noted that the Department of Homeland Security had declined an invitation to appear. The fact that DHS acts like a law unto itself is one of the things that concerns potential neighbors of its biodefense projects.

Edward Hammond of the Sunshine Project testified that over 20,000 people are currently involved in biodefense research, with a twelvefold increase in BSL-4 lab space just since May 2004. Even more BSL-3 lab space has been added; NIH alone (through the National Institute of Allergies and Infectious Diseases, or NIAID) is building fourteen new Regional Biocontainment Laboratories (one of them at the University of Louisville, in my home state). The new construction represented just by major projects, he said, constitutes the equivalent of 36 super Wal-Marts.

Alan Pearson of the Center for Arms Control and Non-Proliferation said annual U.S. bioweapons-related spending rose from $1,327 billion in 2001 to a high of $9,509 billion in 2005. Over $40 billion of new biodefense money had been spent since the 2001 anthrax attacks. (That number has since risen to more than $57 billion.)

Contrary to the bland assurances of biodefense boosters, Dr. Rhodes told the subcommittee there is a "baseline risk" associated with any high-containment germ facility, attributable to human error. The risk is increasing with the expansion, and is greatest at new facilities lacking experience with standard safety protocols. Several witnesses indicated concern that the speed and size of the current expansion are completely overwhelming the supply of trained personnel and the capacity for training others. A lot of new people are researching a lot of new germs: only 15 of the 435 researchers who received NIAID funding from 2001 to 2005 for work on bioweapons agents anthrax, brucellosis, glanders, plague, meliodosis, and tularemia had received funding for the agents before 2001. This resembles suddenly placing crop-duster pilots into the cockpits of Boeing 747s, just because the crop dusters got together and decided to write a grant. And some of the new research—attempts to genetically engineer new pathogens, "aerosol challenges," and "threat assessment research" involving simulated bioweapons attacks—is especially dangerous.

Little Objective Oversight

Even more troubling, the expansion is proceeding more or less mindlessly, with little objective oversight. Several different federal agencies are involved in biodefense research; each has been on its own spending spree, with no one conducting a comprehensive needs-assessment or risk-benefit analysis. A huge new "biodefense campus" at Fort Detrick will feature expanded facilities for the Army and new facilities for Homeland Security, NIAID, CDC, and USDA. The rationale for this BSL-4 megaplex was that having the facilities together in one place would eliminate duplication. Yet the CDC is constructing its own vast new suite of BSL-4 labs; NIAID is building new BSL-4 facilities in Boston and Galveston, and the fourteen Regional Biocontainment laboratories; and DHS and USDA are working together on NBAF. Meanwhile various federal agencies fund a proliferation of biodefense research at our universities, posing a serious threat to whatever academic integrity still remains there, and vastly increasing the odds that a rogue scientist, a foreign terrorist-infiltrator, or a Timothy McVeigh/Unabomber type will get knowledge and state-of-the-art bioweapon agents from our own facilities.

Rhodes said the decentralized, unregulated nature of the expansion means no single federal agency has the mission of tracking the number of new labs, or their aggregate risk. No one is ensuring "that sufficient but not superfluous capacity—that brings with it additional, unnecessary risk—is being created."

All these new facilities get minimal regulatory attention once they're up and running. No single agency in the federal government has primary oversight responsibility. If a facility deals with any of the 72 germs listed by the CDC as select agents, it is subject to some regulation by the CDC or USDA. If a facility engages in genetic engineering of pathogens— recombinant DNA research—and receives NIH funding, it is lightly regulated by the National Institutes of Health. It is expected, then—in theory, if not in practice—to have the recombinant research reviewed by an institutional committee, and to keep minutes of the committee meetings. If a facility doesn't fall within one of these two situations, it may not be regulated at all.

The primary agencies involved with regulation—the CDC, NIH, and USDA—all operate research facilities themselves. This sets up a situation in which the chief regulatory agencies are tempted to downplay the seriousness of safety lapses, to forestall public concern about the safety of their own facilities. This conflict of interest exhibited itself at the subcommittee hearing, where CDC representatives fielded questions both about their oversight of Texas A&M and about a June power loss at the CDC's own suite of new BSL-4 labs. Predictably, both the CDC and NIH representatives suggested the current state of affairs is actually quite safe, thank you.

Rhodes disagreed. Pressed by a Texas congressman who apparently expected a different answer, Rhodes revealed that, in his opinion, the biodefense expansion has made the country less safe than it was before the attacks.

Biodefense: The New Military-Industrial Academic Complex

Even before the FBI formally announced that the 2001 anthrax attacks had been launched from one of our own biodefense facilities, the biodefense boom already seemed yet another knee-jerk war-on-terror overreaction like the Patriot Act and invading Iraq. It is good that a few congressmen examined what biodefense proliferation has wrought, but a strong array of forces remains interested in stoking the bioterror fires and grabbing the funds that are out there: public health, homeland security, and defense agencies enjoying the infusions of new monies; politicians looking for economic development windfalls; research universities already knee-deep in biotech-for-profit conflicts of interest; hometown newspapers who seem to think snagging a biodefense lab is some sort of macho athletic competition. (*Maybe we can mess with Texas for lab site*, the *Athens Banner-Herald* mused just after Athens, Georgia was announced as an NBAF finalist. *This exercise has shown that Kansas can compete with the "big boys,"* said the *Lawrence Journal-World*. Kansas Senator Pat Roberts joined Kentucky Congressman Rogers in likening the NBAF selection process to an NCAA [National Collegiate Athletic Association] basketball tournament: *I think that it's a lot like a Final Four: I think we'll make the cut, and I think we're very well-suited.*)

The economic impact estimates may well be inflated, since they seem to assume pharmaceutical and biotech companies will flock to the occupied regions to exploit the commercial potential of biodefense research. There may be limited demand, though, for vaccines against diseases rarely encountered outside of bioterror scenarios. (Of course, the companies could always take a page out of the anthrax terrorists' playbook and fluff the market with a small bioterror demonstration.) The figures being floated by promoters do demonstrate why this new military-industrial-academic complex will spend any monies, make any outrageous statements, to promote the projects. A University of Georgia study (prepared on behalf of the university's NBAF solicitation) estimated that the overall twenty-year impact of NBAF would be $3.5 billion to $6 billion.

NBAF contenders were willing to plunk down big sums to get a piece of all that. An August 2007 article in the *San Antonio*

Current, an alternative weekly, reported that the Texas NBAF consortium had already spent $500,000 on lawyers and public relations specialists. A December 6, 2006 newspaper article revealed that North Carolina consortium representatives were making twice-weekly trips to Washington to lobby for the NC bid, that they had hired a public relations agency, and that they planned to file as a 501(c)3 nonprofit to seek donations to help cover recruiting costs. Other NBAF finalists probably made similar efforts. Kansas, for instance, set aside $250,000 for lobbying early on, plus another million to defend against a lawsuit brought by the Texas consortium [Kansas won the NBAF project].

Culture of Deception

I became involved in the local struggle against NBAF primarily out of disgust at the deceptions of local boosters and their efforts to ridicule the concerns of opponents. . . .

At first I thought the local deceptions arose out of our peculiar situation: a powerful congressman, a worshipful business community, and a newspaper that kowtowed to both. I eventually learned, however, that similar forces operated in other parts of the country, that Pulaski County had no monopoly on prevarication. This became abundantly clear when I began researching the NBAF finalists. Lies marked the claims not only of politicians and economic development types, but the communications of university academics and the Department of Homeland Security itself.

None of this will surprise anyone who has explored the history of U.S. bioweapons research. Moral norms that arose during World War II and the Cold War are still with us, and fit perfectly into a war-on-terror mindset that sanctioned the ignoring of habeas corpus, the use of secret renditions and torture, and pervasive spying on American citizens. And recent coverups of safety breaches and researcher infections at Boston University and Texas A&M, occurring even as the institutions solicited major new biodefense projects, show clearly that contemporary research universities mirror their biodefense partners' lack of a moral compass.

NBAF public relations efforts have purveyed falsehood in especially reckless fashion. Apparently, the project's huge price tag tempted its promoters to play fast and loose with the truth, and biodefense research itself lacked—and lacks—any culture of integrity that would restrain them.

In August 2008, Americans were reminded that the FBI believed the anthrax attacks of 2001—the events that prompted the current proliferation of new high-risk germ labs—had been launched from within the country's *own* biodefense complex. Not everyone believed those attacks were simply the project of a single crazed researcher.

> "As a result of the strategic planning process, a clear consensus emerged that meeting the goals of the biodefense Research Agendas would require additional research infrastructure."

The Expansion of Biodefense Research Is Necessary

Hugh Auchincloss

In the following viewpoint, Hugh Auchincloss states that the expansion of biodefense research is needed in the wake of terrorist acts and naturally occurring outbreaks. New research objectives, Auchincloss suggests, could not be met with a shortage of Biosafety Level 3 and Biosafety Level 4 laboratories, which are necessary for the study and containment of highly contagious and lethal agents. He asserts that these new facilities are built to the highest standards and accompanied by extended biosafety and biocontainment training efforts—as well as oversight on the protection of human subjects, reporting of accidents, and other facets of research. Auchincloss is the principal deputy director of the National Institute of Allergy and Infectious Diseases.

Hugh Auchincloss, "Protecting the Public Health: The Importance of NIH Biodefense Research Infrastructure," Committee on Energy and Commerce Subcommittee on Oversight and Investigations, United States House of Representatives, October 4, 2007.

As you read, consider the following questions:

1. What facilities account for many existing Biosafety Level 3 locations, according to the author?
2. Who constructs the new facilities, as stated by the author?
3. What is the name of the second-generation smallpox vaccine being developed?

M r. Chairman and members of the Subcommittee, my name is Hugh Auchincloss and I am the Deputy Director of the National Institute of Allergy and Infectious Diseases (NIAID), a component of the National Institutes of Health (NIH), an agency of the Department of Health and Human Services (HHS). I am pleased to have the opportunity to discuss the NIH biodefense research program, including the expansion of the Nation's biodefense research infrastructure and the need to ensure that biodefense research is conducted safely.

The anthrax attacks in 2001 were a sobering reminder that the threat of deliberately released microbes can be used as a form of terrorism. Moreover, naturally occurring microbial outbreaks pose a serious threat to domestic and global health. The experience with SARS [severe acute respiratory syndrome] in 2003 and the ongoing outbreaks of H5N1 avian influenza and extensively drug-resistant tuberculosis have reminded us that defense against naturally emerging microbes must be a top national priority. Congress has recognized the urgency of improving our defenses against emerging public health threats and has supported funding for such research. Within the broad Federal effort against emerging threats to public health, the role of the NIH is to conduct and support basic and applied research that will lead to new vaccines, drugs, and diagnostic tools.

In February 2002, the NIH embarked on a systematic planning process for its biodefense research program. It first convened the Blue Ribbon Panel on Bioterrorism and Its Implications for Biomedical Research, made up of distinguished scientists representing academia, private industry, and government. Based on the panel's advice and extensive discussions with other Federal agencies, the NIH developed three key documents to guide its biodefense research program: the NIAID Strategic Plan for Biodefense Research, the NIAID Research Agenda for Category A Agents, and the NIAID Research Agenda for Category B and C Agents.

Expanding US Biodefense Research Capability

As a result of the strategic planning process, a clear consensus emerged that meeting the goals of the biodefense Research Agendas would require additional research infrastructure, especially research laboratories built to modern Biosafety Level 3 (BSL-3) and Biosafety Level 4 (BSL-4) standards. BSL-3 laboratories are used to study contagious agents that can be transmitted through the air and cause potentially lethal infection. BSL-4 laboratories are used to study agents that pose a high risk of life-threatening disease for which no vaccine or therapy is available; they incorporate all BSL-3 features and occupy safe, isolated zones within a larger building.

There has been considerable discussion of how best to assess the extent of high-containment facilities that would be required in the United States in the public, academic and private sectors and for what purposes these varied facilities are used. Published estimates range from as few as 200 to as many as 1,400 BSL-3 laboratories. (Many institutions maintain multiple facilities.) The explanation for this wide discrepancy is that an assessment of laboratory capacity depends on the definitions and sources of information used. Estimates at the high end, for example, include the many hospitals that maintain small areas that meet BSL-3 standards that can be used for testing clinical samples that might contain infectious agents. These are not "research laboratories." Some hospitals, pharmaceutical companies, biotechnology firms, private reference laboratories and State public health laboratories also have facilities that meet BSL-3 standards, but these are not generally available for NIH-sponsored research. Finally, many BSL-3 facilities constructed before the mid-1990s cannot support research on select agents and on associated animal models. In 2002, NIAID determined that very little usable BSL-3 or BSL-4 research space was actually available for its academic scientists in the extramural research program.

The Blue Ribbon Panel of 2002 noted the shortage of BSL-3 and BSL-4 laboratory space as a significant rate-limiting obstacle in accomplishing the objectives of the NIAID Biodefense Research Agendas. In response, NIAID estimated the new BSL-3 and BSL-4 facilities that would be required to accomplish the Research Agenda. Congress also recognized the critical need for new BSL-3/4 laboratories and responded quickly to supply the necessary resources to fulfill this need. In 2002, the Department of Defense and Emergency Supplemental Appropriations for Recovery from and Response to Terrorist Attacks on the United States Act, Public Law (P.L.) 107-117, appropriated $70 million for the construction and renovation of NIH intramural biocontainment facilities. The Consolidated Appropriations Act of 2003, P.L. 108-7, provided $372.6 million to NIAID for construction of extramural biocontainment facilities and $291 million for construction of additional intramural biocontainment facilities. Further, the Project BioShield Act of 2004 (P.L. 108-276), amended the Public Health Service Act to provide ongoing authority to NIAID to award grants and contracts for construction of research facilities. An additional $150 million was appropriated for NIAID in the 2005 Consolidated Appropriations Act (P.L. 108-447) for extramural facilities construction grants.

The NIH is now implementing a construction program that will complete 14 new BSL-3 facilities and 4 new BSL-4 facilities within the next several years. During this process, the NIH or its funded institutions have participated in literally hundreds of public forums on the nature and safety of the new facilities, and have submitted reports to Congress annually, along with periodic updates on our strategic plans. In addition, NIH leadership has discussed the infrastructure expansion with Congress on many occasions. And because NIH does not fund or conduct classified research, the title and substance of every research project funded by the NIH is publicly available.

Another important aspect of the biodefense research infrastructure is a network of ten NIH-funded Regional Centers of Excellence for Biodefense and Emerging Infectious Diseases Research (RCEs). Created in 2003, these multidisciplinary academic research programs are located at institutions across the country and provide the scientific expertise for a wide-ranging biodefense research program, directed against deliberate and naturally-occurring threats, that will be pursued in the new facilities.

NIH's Role in Ensuring Safety

The NIH is committed to helping ensure that all biodefense research facilities provide maximum protection for public health. The NIH is committed to the highest quality in the design and construction of these facilities, the rigorous training of the personnel that operate them, and the safe conduct of the research undertaken within them.

To ensure that the new laboratories are designed and constructed to the highest standards, the NIAID works closely with each grantee institution. Highly experienced NIAID staff architects and engineers, with extensive experience in design of biocontainment facilities, are assisted by a Construction Quality Management group of contracted consultants with additional expertise. Together, these teams make certain that the finished projects will meet the regulations of HHS's Centers for Disease Control and Prevention (CDC) and the Department of Agriculture's Animal and Plant Health Inspection Service (USDA/APHIS) for facilities that conduct research on select agents.

The NIH also supports a vigorous biosafety and biocontainment training effort that has expanded substantially over the past five years. The National Biosafety and Biocontainment Training Program (NBBTP) is a partnership between the NIAID and the NIH Division of Occupational Health and Safety (DOHS), managed by a not-for-profit education and research foundation. The mission of this program is to prepare biosafety and biocontainment professionals of the highest caliber. The program offers two-year post-baccalaureate and post-doctoral fellowships at NIH's campus in Bethesda, Maryland, with both academic and hands-on training. The NBBTP has also provided training for containment laboratory operation and maintenance personnel across the country. In addition to this program, NIAID funds 28 Institutional Training Grants in Biodefense, and the RCEs conduct extensive training in biosafety and biocontainment. At the RCE at Emory University in Atlanta, for example, trainees from across the country regularly participate in BSL-3 and BSL-4 training in mock laboratories, constructed specifically for training purposes.

When these new facilities are ready for operation, NIH is committed to ensuring that the research conducted within them is performed safely. The most widely used guidance on the safe conduct of this research is the Biosafety in Microbiological and Biomedical Laboratories Manual (BMBL), which was first produced jointly in 1984 by the NIH and CDC and which is now in its fifth edition and available online.

Monitoring adherence to good laboratory practices is a complex process because multiple agencies are involved. Much of the research in BSL-3 and BSL-4 facilities involves pathogens that have been designated as select agents. CDC and APHIS have the responsibility for regulating the possession, use, and transfer of select agents. For research that involves recombinant DNA, the select agent regulations incorporate the NIH Guidelines for Research Involving Recombinant DNA Molecules (Recombinant DNA Guidelines) as a consideration in the entity's development of its biosafety plan. The NIH Office of Biotechnology Activities (OBA), with advice and guidance from the NIH Recombinant

DNA Advisory Committee (RAC), is responsible for implementation of the Recombinant DNA Guidelines, which outlines biosafety and containment standards for research involving recombinant DNA. Also, the select agent regulations require that restricted experiments, such as the deliberate transfer of a drug-resistant trait to a select agent, must be approved by CDC or APHIS prior to initiation. However, some research conducted in BSL-3 facilities involves neither select agents nor recombinant DNA.

Oversight by Local Institutional Bodies

Local institutional bodies play a very important role in oversight of many aspects of biomedical research. For example, oversight to protect human subjects in clinical studies is provided by local Institutional Review Boards (IRBs), and in the case of animal research, oversight to ensure humane treatment is provided by the Institutional Animal Care and Use Committees (IACUCs). The NIH Guidelines mandate that Institutional Biosafety Committees (IBCs) oversee recombinant DNA research, but many institutions have gradually broadened IBC responsibilities to include oversight of research involving all pathogens studied at BSL-3 and BSL-4 levels. At this time there is no federal body that sets national standards or policies for this function of local IBCs, and adherence to BMBL guidelines for BSL-3 and BSL-4 research is voluntary; however, the select agents regulations require regulated entities to comply with the BMBL guidelines or equivalent standards.

The NIH is deeply concerned about recent reports of accidents occurring in BSL-3 facilities. When these events involve recombinant DNA, they are reported to the OBA, and a root cause analysis is done so that NIH can assess the adequacy of the institution's response and work with the institution to put mechanisms in place to mitigate the chance of a reoccurrence. To enhance all of the functions of the IBCs, the NIH has worked intensively with the IBC community. These efforts have included an extensive program of outreach and education, involving frequent day-long training sessions, exhibits at major scientific conferences, policy guidances, educational resources for institutions to use in local training, and other means. Furthermore, each of the institutions receiving one of the new facilities construction grants from NIAID has an IBC appropriately registered with NIH and each has willingly accepted responsibility for adhering to BMBL standards.

The NIH is examining ways to strengthen local and federal oversight of facilities that conduct NIH-funded research. The issues associated with oversight of research in BSL-3 and BSL-4 facilities transcend the NIH, or even the HHS. Biodefense research involving BSL-3 and BSL-4 facilities is conducted by many government agencies, including the Department of Defense (DoD), the Department of Homeland Security (DHS), and the USDA, as well as by universities and biotechnology companies. As I noted earlier, BSL-3 facilities exist in hospitals for routine handling of clinical samples. It is important to devise a framework that improves oversight, training, and reporting to enhance safety without causing unintended negative consequences for either patient care or the biodefense research program. For that reason, HHS, USDA, DHS, and DoD have already agreed to establish a Trans-Federal Task Force to undertake, in consultation with other relevant agencies, an intensive analysis of the current biosafety framework and to develop a set of recommendations for improvement. Given the critical importance of biosafety to protecting public health and the concerns that the high containment facilities engender among local communities, active participation in this process from the public at large will be essential.

Support for Biodefense Research Is Essential

Support for infrastructure for biodefense research is essential if we are to fulfill our biodefense research agenda and protect the Nation from disease threats, be they deliberate or acts of nature. We have already made substantial progress with the facilities now available. For example, NIH-funded scientists have developed a safer second-generation smallpox vaccine called ACAM2000 and a very promising new smallpox drug named ST-246. Investigators have developed and tested a new anthrax vaccine called rPA and have achieved promising results with antibodies capable of neutralizing anthrax toxins. They have developed first- and second-generation vaccines against Ebola virus, and investigated a promising Ebola therapy based on RNA interference. These and many other advances required the use of containment facilities of the type that are now under construction. Progress should occur more rapidly as the new facilities become available.

NIH-funded biodefense researchers are acutely aware of the threat posed by the pathogens they study. These experts understand the need to handle them with utmost care, the need for rigorous training and state-of-the-art equipment, and the need to scrupulously follow all required procedures. Their awareness also includes a deep understanding that the Nation's biosecurity depends on their work, which is the conduct of research that will lead to new tools essential to meet emerging and re-emerging threats to public health.

> *"No one agency is responsible for determining, or able to determine, the aggregate or cumulative risks associated with the expansion of these high-containment laboratories."*

The Expansion of Biodefense Research Requires More Oversight

Nancy Kingsbury

In the following viewpoint, author Nancy Kingsbury calls for increased oversight for the proliferation of biodefense research. Since its initial expansion, the author maintains, no federal agency has been designated to track the increasing number of high-containment laboratories and, therefore, is unable to determine the risks involved and whether the current capacity falls short of, meets, or exceeds a level of national security. Kingsbury defends the safety record of these facilities but claims that several incidents demonstrate weaknesses in the systems and procedures of biodefense research. Kingsbury is the managing director of Applied Research and Methods, which provides technical and specialist expertise to the US Government Accountability Office.

Nancy Kingsbury, "Testimony Before the Subcommittee on Oversight and Investigations, Committee on Energy and Commerce, House of Representatives: High-Containment Libraries, National Strategy for Oversight Is Needed," September 22, 2009. www.gao.gov /htext/d091036t.html.

As you read, consider the following questions:

1. How does the author characterize the initial expansion of high-containment laboratories?
2. Why do accidents at high-containment laboratories occur, in Kingsbury's view?
3. Why is a consistent supply of electrical power essential to high-containment laboratories?

We are pleased to be here to discuss our report on a national strategy for high-containment laboratories that deal with dangerous pathogens—also known as biosafety level-3 (BSL-3) laboratories and biosafety level-4 (BSL-4) laboratories—in the United States, which was released yesterday. The number of high-containment laboratories working with dangerous biological pathogens have proliferated in recent years. In 2007, we reported on several issues associated with the proliferation of high-containment laboratories in the United States, including risks posed by biosafety incidents that have occurred in the past. The Federal Bureau of Investigation's allegation in August 2008 that a scientist at the U.S. Army Medical Research Institute of Infectious Diseases was the sole perpetrator of the 2001 anthrax attacks raised additional concerns about the possibility of insider misuse of high-containment laboratory facilities, material, and technology. The public is concerned about these laboratories because the deliberate or accidental release of biological agents can have disastrous consequences by exposing workers and the public to dangerous pathogens. Highly publicized laboratory errors and controversies about where high-containment laboratories should be located have raised questions about whether the governing framework, oversight, and standards for biosafety and biosecurity measures are adequate. In this context, you asked us to address the following questions:

1. To what extent, and in what areas, has the number of high-containment laboratories increased in the United States?

2. Which federal agency is responsible for tracking the expansion of high-containment laboratories and determining the associated aggregate risks?
3. What lessons can be learned from highly publicized incidents at high-containment laboratories and actions taken by the regulatory agencies?

To answer these questions, we interviewed federal agency officials as well as experts in microbiology, reviewed literature, conducted site visits, and surveyed 12 federal agencies to determine if they have a mission to track high-containment laboratories in the United States. We also interviewed officials from relevant intelligence agencies to determine if they have a mission to determine insider risks in high-containment laboratories. The expert panel that reviewed this report comprised scientists with substantive expertise in microbiological and select agent research and the operation of high-containment laboratories.

We conducted our work from September 2005 through June 2009 in accordance with generally accepted government auditing standards. Those standards require that we plan and perform the audit to obtain sufficient, appropriate evidence to provide a reasonable basis for our findings and conclusions based on our audit objectives. We believe that the evidence obtained provides a reasonable basis for our findings and conclusions based on our audit objectives.

The Number of High-Containment Laboratories Is Increasing

We found that since 2001, the number of BSL-4 and BSL-3 laboratories in the United States has increased, and this expansion has taken place across federal, state, academic, and private sectors and throughout the United States. Federal officials and experts believe that while the number of BSL-4 laboratories in the United States is known, the number of BSL-3 laboratories is unknown. Information about the number, location, activities, and ownership is available for high-containment laboratories that are registered with the Centers for Disease Control and Prevention's (CDC) Division of Select Agents and Toxins (DSAT) or the United States Department of Agriculture's (USDA) Animal and Plant Health and Inspection Service (APHIS) select agent programs, but not for those outside the program. The recent expansion of high-containment laboratories in the United States began in response to the need to develop medical countermeasures and better risk evaluations after the anthrax attacks in 2001. Understandably, the expansion initially lacked a clear, governmentwide coordinated strategy. In that emergency situation, the expansion was based on individual agency perceptions of requirements relative to the capacity their high-containment labs required as well as the availability of congressionally appropriated funding. Decisions to fund the construction of high-containment labs were made by multiple federal agencies in multiple budget cycles. Federal and state agencies, academia, and the private sector considered their individual requirements, but an assessment of national needs was lacking. Even now, after more than 7 years, GAO [the US Government Accountability Office] was unable to find any projections based on a governmentwide strategic evaluation of future capacity requirements set in light of existing capacity; the numbers, locations, and missions of the laboratories needed to effectively counter biothreats; and national public health goals. Such information is needed to ensure that the United States will have facilities in the right place with the right specifications.

No Federal Agency Regulates US Biosafety

Currently, no executive or legislative mandate directs any federal agency to track the expansion of all high-containment laboratories. Because no federal agency has the mission to track the expansion of BSL-3 and BSL-4 laboratories in the United States, no federal agency knows how many such laboratories exist in the

United States. While there is a consensus among federal agency officials and experts that some degree of risk is always associated with high-containment laboratories, no one agency is responsible for determining, or able to determine, the aggregate or cumulative risks associated with the expansion of these high-containment laboratories. As a consequence, no federal agency can determine whether high-containment laboratory capacity may now meet or exceed the national need or is at a level that can be operated safely.

The Risks of High-Containment Laboratories

Four highly publicized incidents in high-containment laboratories, as well as evidence in the scientific literature, demonstrate that (1) while laboratory accidents are rare, they do occur, primarily because of human error or systems (management and technical operations) failure, including the failure of safety equipment and procedures; (2) insiders can pose a risk; and (3) it is difficult to control inventories of biological agents with currently available technologies. It has been suggested that personnel reliability programs would mitigate the insider risk. The National Science Advisory Board for Biosecurity reported that there is little evidence that personnel reliability measures are effective or have predictive value in identifying individuals who may pose an insider risk. (4) Continuity of electrical power is vital for the safe functioning of high-containment laboratories, in particular since maintenance of essential pressure differentials using electrically driven fans provides an important barrier for preventing the uncontrolled release of agents. Lapses in electrical power that occurred at a CDC laboratory raise concerns about standards in high-containment laboratory facility design, management of construction, and operations.

Taken as a whole, these incidents demonstrate failures of systems and procedures meant to maintain biosafety in high-containment laboratories. For example, they revealed the failure to comply with regulatory requirements, safety measures that were not commensurate with the level of risk to public health posed by laboratory workers and pathogens in the laboratories, and the failure to fund ongoing facility maintenance and monitor the operational effectiveness of laboratory physical infrastructure.

The Development of a Strategic Plan

Oversight plays a critical role in improving biosafety and ensuring that high-containment laboratories comply with regulations. However, some aspects of the current oversight programs provided by the Departments of Health and Human Services and Agriculture are dependent upon entities monitoring themselves and reporting incidents to federal regulators. Since 2001, personnel reliability programs have been established to counter insider risks, but their cost, effectiveness, and programmatic impact have not been evaluated.

In conclusion, proliferation of high-containment laboratories is taking place in all sectors. Furthermore, since no single agency is in charge of the current expansion, no one is determining the associated aggregate risks posed by the expansion. As a consequence, no federal agency can determine whether high-containment laboratory capacity may now be less than, meet, or exceed the national need or is at a level that can be operated safely.

If an agency was tasked or a mechanism was established with the purpose of overseeing the expansion of high-containment laboratories, it could develop a strategic plan to (1) ensure that the number and capabilities of potentially dangerous high-containment laboratories are no greater or less than necessary, (2) balance the risks and benefits of expanding such laboratories, and (3) determine the type of oversight needed.

Such an agency or mechanism could analyze the biothreat problems that need to be addressed by additional BSL-3 and -4 laboratories, the scientific and technical capabilities and containment features that such laboratories need to have, how the laboratories should be distributed geographically, and how the activities of the laboratories would be coordinated to achieve intended goals. The agency or mechanism responsible for overseeing the expansion of high-containment laboratories could also be responsible for coordinating with the scientific community to develop guidelines for high-containment laboratory design, construction, and commissioning and training standards for laboratory workers; providing definitions for exposure; developing appropriate inventory control measures; and providing guidance on the most efficient approach to personnel reliability programs.

Overall, the safety record of high-containment laboratories has been good, although a number of weaknesses have become apparent over time. Consequently, along with expansion there needs to be a commensurate development of both operational and oversight procedures to address known deficiencies and, as far as practicable, proactively evaluate future risks.

Laboratory operators, in collaboration with regulators, need to develop and work through potential failure scenarios and use that information to develop and put in place mechanisms to challenge procedures, systems, and equipment to ensure continuing effectiveness.

Recommendations for Executive Action

To address these issues, we recommended that the National Security Advisor, in consultation with the Secretaries of Health and Human Services (HHS), Agriculture, Defense (DOD), and Homeland Security (DHS); the National Intelligence Council; and other executive departments as deemed appropriate identify a single entity charged with periodic governmentwide strategic evaluation of high-containment laboratories that will:

1. determine:

   • the number, locations, and mission of the laboratories needed to effectively meet national goals to counter biothreats,

- the existing capacity within the United States,
- the aggregate risks associated with the laboratories' expansion, and
- the type of oversight needed, and

2. develop, in consultation with the scientific community, national standards for the design, construction, commissioning, and operation of high-containment laboratories, specifically including provisions for long-term maintenance.

We recommended that the Secretaries of HHS and USDA develop (1) a clear definition of exposure to select agents and (2) a mechanism for sharing lessons learned from reported laboratory accidents so that best practices—for other operators of high-containment laboratories—can be identified.

Should the Secretaries consider implementing a personnel reliability program for high-containment laboratories to deal with insider risk, we recommended that they evaluate and document the cost, effectiveness, and programmatic impact of such a program.

Recognizing that biological agent inventories cannot be completely controlled at present, we also recommended that the Secretaries of HHS and USDA review existing inventory control systems and invest in and develop appropriate technologies to minimize the potential for insider misuse of biological agents.

> *"Development of countermeasures to natural infectious disease would offer direct benefits for biodefense efforts—far greater than those that, conversely, would accrue to infectious diseases prevention from biodefense research."*

Infectious Disease Research Should Be Pursued Instead of Biodefense Research

Lynn C. Klotz and Edward J. Sylvester

In the following viewpoint excerpted from Breeding Bio Insecurity, *Lynn C. Klotz and Edward J. Sylvester argue that natural outbreaks and pandemics pose a greater threat than bioterrorism, and call for more research on infectious diseases. For example, the flu, drug-resistant bacteria, and staph infections kill tens of thousands of people annually, Klotz and Sylvester point out. Also, the authors propose that the fifty-fifty chance of a large-scale anthrax attack is statistically much lower than the probability of an influenza pandemic. They advise that research and development funding be directed toward infectious diseases, which can advance biodefense efforts. Klotz, a biotechnology consultant, and Sylvester, a science*

Lynn C. Klotz and Edward J. Sylvester, "Chapter Eight: All Roads Lead to Public Health," *Breeding Bio Insecurity: How US Biodefense Is Exporting Fear, Globalizing Risk, and Making Us All Less Secure.* Chicago: University of Chicago Press, 2009, pp. 151–158. All rights reserved. Reproduced by permission.

journalist, are coauthors of Breeding Bio Insecurity: How US Biodefense Is Exporting Fear, Globalizing Risk, and Making Us All Less Secure.

As you read, consider the following questions:
1. As offered by Klotz and Sylvester, what are the funding implications of how the government currently assesses the likelihood and consequences of bioweapons and infectious diseases?
2. What estimation for deaths worldwide do Klotz and Sylvester provide for the next pandemic influenza?
3. What is the argument of those who support huge biodefense budgets, in the authors' opinion?

To us, biosecurity means safeguarding from infectious disease in all its manifestations. That requires committing the largest portion of our finite resources to shielding against the threats most likely to kill us. Protection against bioweaponry is just one element in such a shield, but in the wake of the Amerithrax [anthrax] attacks [of 2001] and the government's hasty and overblown response, this highly unlikely threat to American life has become the squeaky wheel, garnering billions in appropriations, cornering the market on public fear, and capturing the news spotlight.

We must ask ourselves what biological threats pose the greatest danger to our families. Biowarfare is well down the list of probables . . . we can now put some force behind our claims for the low risk of a major anthrax attack, the kind that could truly disrupt public life and would require a major public health response, in comparison with looming health threats such as a pandemic flu and the steady, year-in, year-out toll of annual diseases like drug-resistant staph infections and garden-variety influenza.

Now the government assesses the relative likelihood and consequences of bioweapons, pandemic flu, and annual infectious disease threats in three different "boxes" so the yearly threats never get compared to bioweapons. That means the most powerful or emotionally charged concern wins in the ensuing funding battles. Efforts against bioweaponry and pandemic flu are funded from special vaults provided under BioShield 2004, the Bush administration's $6.1 billion pandemic flu plan, and other dedicated sources. That leaves the killers and disablers of the largest number of Americans still wanting for additional research funding. Only a combined risk assessment makes sense to determine a health hazard's true impact. . . .

Varying Predictions

We're using the term "risk" as an indicator of the seriousness of a threat to us, arrived at by multiplying the consequences of the threat by the probability of occurrence. Since our crude assessment considers only fatalities—in order to make the point that our priorities are skewed—some of our conclusions are only a first word on the subject, not the last. Let's take annual flu as the standard against which other threats are measured. Flu kills around thirty-six thousand people every year, so deaths in the tens of thousands occur each year with certainty—that is, with a probability of one. Another group of particularly deadly disease agents, the feared hospital-borne multiple drug-resistant (MDR) bacteria, kill tens of thousands every year, again a certainty. A recent report places deaths from just one of these bacteria, methicillin-resistant Staphylococcus aureus, at over eighteen thousand per year, an annual death toll greater than that of AIDS.

Let's add into the mix the possibility of a pandemic flu, now a big worry, which is distinct from the annual flu. But how can we rationally assess the threat of a bioweapons attack that has never happened against that of a global flu outbreak that recurs, if infrequently, and annual infectious diseases? The fact is that it must be done for simple reasons. We mount bulwarks against all manner of biological threats—from AIDS, tuberculosis, and

other infectious diseases to biowarfare—and we do so from a fund of limited resources that we must spend efficiently.

Without a data-based ballpark calculation of the threat and size of a new pandemic flu, even experts can make wildly varying predictions. Here is the assessment of Robert Webster, not only an eminent virologist but director of the WHO [World Health Organization] Collaborating Center on the Ecology of Influenza Viruses in Lower Animals and Birds: "The world is teetering on the edge of a pandemic that could kill a large fraction of the human population," he wrote recently in a co-authored article. Recalling the 1997 virus that spread through Hong Kong poultry markets, Webster said, "the only thing that saved us was the quick thinking of scientists who convinced health authorities to slaughter more than a million domesticated fowl in the city's markets. The avian virus turned out to be a new strain—one that the human population had never seen before. These deadly new strains arise a few times every century, and the next one may arrive any day now" Webster believes the 1918-like scenario will replay. "But this time it will be worse."

Michael Osterholm, director of the Center for Infectious Disease Research and Policy at the University of Minnesota, agrees. He foresees a toll of some 270 million pandemic flu deaths worldwide, a number he arrived at simply by extrapolating the 1918 death toll of 40 million to the world's current population.

Scary stuff, but now listen to Paul Offit of Children's Hospital of Philadelphia and the University of Pennsylvania School of Medicine. He says of avian flu, "the virus is clearly not so highly contagious among mammals, and I just don't think it's going to become so." Moreover, Offit does not expect the next pandemic until sometime around 2025.

The WHO itself takes a conservative position, estimating that a new pandemic would take the lives of from 2 million to 7.4 million people, believing that the 1918 pandemic was unusual and unlikely to be repeated.

Probabilities of an Anthrax Attack

We will try to make rational risk assessments about pandemic flu and anthrax as best we can in a field of such uncertain numbers. Since anthrax is on everyone's minds, we'll tackle it first. . . . A bioweapons assault resulting in thirty thousand fatalities is a reasonable guess for a large attack, so we will use it. What is the probability of an attack of this magnitude in any given year? Is it .001? Or .01? Or a radical 0.1—meaning that there is a one in ten chance of an attack in the coming year? We must make some choice, because everyone's risk assessments are based on guesses of such probabilities. But what does each one mean in everyday terms?

Our intuitive method involves simply thinking about the number of years that must go by to have a 50-50 chance of such an attack, given its probability in any one year. . . .

To set the probability of such an anthrax attack at 0.1 would mean there is a 50-50 chance that in 6.6 years we will have suffered at least one such attack resulting in 30,000 fatalities. Given what we showed would be required to mount such an offensive, that probability would be unrealistic. Only the most fearful among us would believe this to represent the seriousness of the anthrax threat today. How about the lowest probability, 0.001? We could then expect 692 years to pass before there was a 50-50 chance of at least one attack, and clearly one would have to be blissfully optimistic to pretend we are that safe. Any realistic guess must lie in between, so let's look at 0.01 probability, meaning that 69.9 years will pass before there is a 50-50 chance that an attack has occurred. This, too, seems optimistic, although it seems more realistic, given the 30,000 fatalities that would mark an extremely successful bioweapons attack.

Consider a higher probability: 0.03. Arbitrary, but since we have no way of knowing the real numbers, this seems a reasonable guess. At this probability, we should expect about 23 years to go by to reach even odds that we will have suffered at least one attack. It means that the likelihood-weighted fatalities in any one year would be 900, the product of 0.03 probability and the 30,000 deaths used for the threat assessment. That's more fatalities than the annual toll of tuberculosis but still quite a bit fewer than deaths from multiple drug-resistant staph infection, garden-variety flu, and others. One conclusion is obvious: more funding for such annual infectious diseases could save far more lives. Interestingly, that would remain true even if we had used that unrealistically high probability of 0.1 and extreme fatalities of 150,000. The risk adjusted fatalities would number 15,000, and the conclusion would not change.

To arrive at truly realistic probabilities for these attacks would require better worldwide intelligence than we have seen or probably will. We would need to know how close rogue nations are to developing and delivering bioweapons and their plans for using them, as well as whether terrorist groups have the agents and are capable of delivering them to cause mass deaths. On the other hand, if we were to get solid intelligence about plans for a particular attack, the odds estimation would become much more concrete.

Precisely or not, we have to assess threats to plan for countermeasures we want to have in the Strategic National Stockpile ten to fifteen years from now. Decades of experience in new drug development by pharmaceutical companies shows that it can take that long to discover, develop, and produce new countermeasures.

Considering Influenza

Now consider influenza—not the garden variety but the kind of severe pandemic we know can kill many millions. We estimate that the next pandemic will claim 36 million victims worldwide, about the number of deaths from the devastating 1918 pandemic. This death toll is higher than the conservative WHO estimate but far lower than Osterholm's, so it strikes a balance. There is also some statistical justification for using this particular number, which is the logarithmic average of the WHO's and Osterholm's projections.

The U.S. population of 300 million is about 4.6 percent of the world's 6.5 billion, so we will estimate the number of U.S. deaths at 1.7 million—although America probably would not suffer as great a loss of life as developing countries. For the chances that such a devastating outbreak will occur in any one year, some real data are available from the actual influenza pandemics of 1918, 1957, and 1968 and if the next pandemic had started as we did this projection (2007) it would be recurring an average of every 29.7 years. Granted that a total of three pandemics in a century provides meager data, but they are certainly better than the data for anthrax, which are nonexistent. So we will estimate the probability of such a flu pandemic in any year as one in 29.7, or 1/29.7=0.034 yearly probability. That would put the likelihood weighted yearly U.S. fatalities at 57,200—representing 0.034 times 1.7 million. That is more than the yearly toll of any single infectious disease and about a third of the 177,000 fatalities from all infectious diseases in the United States. The bottom line is that the government is clearly on the right track in committing large-scale funding to research and development of pandemic flu countermeasures. However, there are concerns over how those funds are being used. Too much money has been spent on Tamiflu, a drug that may not work on pandemic flu, and . . . more money is urgently needed at state and local levels to improve sorely needed surge capacity at hospitals.

Out of Proportion and Misdirected

Some argue that a massive bioweapons attack would heavily damage our national security, so we must counter even the slimmest of possibilities with concomitantly massive funding. In this view, virtually any amount of spending on biodefense is justified, and comparisons with budgets for annual infectious diseases are irrelevant.

Those who justify such biodefense budgets further argue that Congress, which appropriated the massive amounts for bioweapons countermeasures, has judged such funding levels appropriate and is simply carrying out the will of the people.

On strategic grounds, [former White House science and security analyst] Gerald Epstein points out, "A nation's security infrastructure exists to protect its citizens' lives, but that has never been its sole responsibility. More generally, it exists to preserve objectives that include national sovereignty and freedom of action." He further adds, "Policies that preserved the lives of every American citizen but ceded control over U.S. foreign policy to others would be rejected by any American political leader."

We agree. But deflecting badly needed new funding away from infectious diseases with their high yearly morbidity and mortality and from such growing threats as antibiotic-resistant bacteria in order to bolster bioweapons defense also represents an obvious national security cost. [Social medicine professor] Victor Sidel sums up: "In short, bioterrorism preparedness programs have been a disaster for public health."

As we have shown, our massive biodefense-focused spending is out of proportion to the current threat. Of equal importance, much of it is misdirected. Development of countermeasures to natural infectious disease would offer direct benefits for biodefense efforts—far greater than those that, conversely, would accrue to infectious diseases prevention from biodefense research.

We can have our cake and eat it too—by funding research and countermeasure development for natural infectious diseases and keeping a sharp eye out for the many potential biodefense spinoffs.

> "The anthrax letters case, bio-lab accidents and security breaches reported in the last several years make clear that the specific and repeatedly dismissed health, safety, and environmental concerns communities have raised are real."

Biodefense Research Should Account for Citizens' Concerns

Biological Weapons Prevention Project

In the following viewpoint, the Biological Weapons Prevention Project (BWPP) writes that citizens' concerns regarding the expansion of biodefense laboratories should not be dismissed. According to to BWPP, communities have raised the following issues: Flawed risk assessments on environmental effects, accidents, the lack of effective regulation and transparency, and questionable definitions of acceptable risk. The project recommends an integrated federal policy to coordinate biodefense programs, demilitarization of research, and a moratorium on new laboratories. Launched in 2003 by nongovernmental organizations, BWPP is a global network that aims to eliminate the weaponization of diseases.

Biological Weapons Prevention Project, "Biodefense Research and Development Policy in 2009: A Citizen Perspective," May 2009.

As you read, consider the following questions:

1. According to BWPP, what has not been taken into account when siting laboratories?
2. What have communities been told about the likelihood of accidents, as alleged by BWPP?
3. What has occurred when communities attempt to obtain information about biodefense laboratories, as stated by BWPP?

We, the undersigned, face the reality or prospect of federally funded high containment biodefense labs being situated in our communities. We represent citizen groups from many localities throughout the U.S. who have specific health, safety and environmental concerns about their presence in our neighborhoods and cities. We are united in our belief that the proliferation of these laboratories represents a significant threat not just to our communities, but also to our nation, and the world. We agree with Biological Weapons Convention non-proliferation experts that we risk creating a biowarfare arms race with those who do not trust and cannot verify U.S. intentions. The spread of these labs makes us all less safe.

Since the August 2008 revelations that the 2001 anthrax letters originated from within the premier U.S. biodefense lab, it has become tragically clear that Congress must move quickly to re-evaluate the nation's biodefense programs. We share many concerns about the expansion of Bio-Safety Level [BSL] 3 and 4 laboratories in federal facilities, and in the hundreds of poorly regulated or unregulated academic and private sector laboratories around the country.

Concerns of Communities

Failure to acknowledge community concerns. We have tried in numerous ways to call attention to problems of community safety and the limited roles afforded citizens in communities where laboratories are proposed and sited. And we have experienced years of dismissive responses to these concerns from those promoting and funding laboratory expansion. The anthrax letters case, bio-lab accidents and security breaches reported in the last several years make clear that the specific and repeatedly dismissed health, safety, and environmental concerns communities have raised are real and require a more adequate response.

Flawed risk assessments. In each of our communities, we have found that environmental impacts and hazards associated with these labs have not been analyzed with thoroughness, clarity and scientific rigor. It is not possible to mitigate unacknowledged risks. In particular, we have been appalled by the failure to take environmental justice considerations into account in siting laboratories. Additionally, there has been inadequate community input to the planning and design of risk assessments, resulting in assessments that do not reflect community concerns.

Accidents. Initially we were told that there was virtually no possibility of accidents in high containment labs; it has become clear however that many laboratory accidents have occurred and many have gone unreported. This is demonstrated by the tularemia infections at Boston University, revealed by a whistle blower, and the Brucella infections at Texas A&M, uncovered by the Sunshine Project. The CDC [Centers for Disease Control and Prevention] has records on more than 100 reported accidents in the past several years in Level 3 and 4 labs.

Lack of effective regulation. It has also become clear that laboratory regulation and oversight are poor, as detailed by the Government Accountability Office in 2007 and 2008. The GAO reports that safety programs and protocols are inadequate and have not been followed with consistency and rigor. Many private and academic BSL-3 laboratories are essentially unregulated.

Lack of transparency. Transparency is a prerequisite for effective oversight, for establishing trust with communities and with others who may not trust the intentions of the United States. It is required to make the Biological Weapons Convention a viable treaty. Yet the work conducted in U.S. biodefense labs is not transparent. Despite great effort, community groups have been unable to obtain vital information about what is actually happening or planned for these laboratories. Security concerns are used as an excuse to restrict citizen access to reports of ongoing or planned studies. FOIA [Freedom of Information Act] requests about accidents and the minutes of Institutional Biosafety Committee meetings are routinely denied.

Defining acceptable risks. "Low-probability" but "high-consequence" accidents that could result in a public health disaster in our communities are of great concern. Who decides what is an acceptable level of risk? Should an academic institution, a corporation, or a federal agency decide what is acceptable risk for the at-risk citizens?

Concerns Extend Beyond Individual Communities

Dangerous growth in labs and workers handling select agents. We are sobered by the fact that since the anthrax letter attacks, the number of workers in these labs has grown from a small number to over 16,000; bio-safety laboratory space has grown up to twenty-fold since 2001. Yet by most accounts, including the GAO and the World at Risk report, the "unbridled increase" in research and development with bio-warfare pathogens has made the world less safe.

Poor research agenda oversight. The research agenda of U.S. biodefense programs has also expanded greatly in the wake of the 2001 anthrax letters. Who sets priorities for biodefense research? For example, who decided it was acceptable to genetically

Communication Is Inherently Difficult

If there is an accident, who will lab officials contact in the community and under what circumstances? How will lab officials work with the county public health officer? Who has authority to determine when quarantine is required? Who do local doctors and ER staff contact at the labs if they think they are dealing with laboratory acquired infection? How would these local doctors even know, particularly in the case of a novel pathogen? . . . These questions are relevant to all communities in proximity to biodefense labs.

And yes, we continue to grapple with the massive inequity of power between powerful, mission-driven bureaucracies and local communities. Communication is inherently difficult between two these very different worlds. Lab officials are clear that they believe additional information about lab safety will address citizen "fearfulness." The community sees this characterization as dismissive of the specific issues we have raised and avoids the establishment of a real role for elected officials and citizens in addressing public health and safety.

Beth Willis, "The Lab in My Backyard,"
GeneWatch, *April 16, 2010.*

recreate, transport, and do research on the formerly extinct 1918 flu virus, regardless of the risks involved? There are far too many comparable examples.

Misplaced funding priorities. Since 2001, there has been an exponential increase in funding for biodefense research on exotic pathogens posing theoretical risks, while funding for infectious disease research has declined slightly. In 2005, more than 750 scientists, including Nobel Prize-winners, decried the diversion of funds to biodefense programs away from vital and pressing research of broad applicability on infectious diseases and pandemics.

Dual-use research hazards. We are concerned about the threats associated with exotic, genetically modified pathogens, which can serve as bio-weapons agents. Dual-use research is either offensive or defensive, based only upon intent. Much BSL-3 and BSL-4 research is dual-use by its very nature, which increases the risk of misuse, and can raise serious questions about U.S. compliance with the Biological Weapons Convention.

Risk of internal sabotage. Now we also know that the possibility of internal sabotage is quite real. We have been told officially that both the weaponized anthrax and the perpetrator of the only bio-terror attack in our history came from within the U.S. biodefense program.

Creating a New Model for Biodefense
We cannot afford to simply continue the uncritical biodefense building boom of the last eight years.

We need an integrated, coherent federal policy. Since 2001, biodefense funding has provided a $57 billion economic boon, much of it for the private sector. Biodefense programs are spread among many federal departments. However, according to the GAO and others these programs are frequently duplicative and poorly coordinated. We have seen no evidence of an integrated federal policy, still less one openly debated by Congress. Congress needs to evaluate current research and development priorities, funding levels and research requirements in relation to verifiable threats to human and livestock health. Our country needs a fact-based assessment of biological threats, both natural and man-made.

We need to demilitarize biomedical research. We are aware that intense debate is taking place within the scientific community about whether or not much of the current biodefense research agenda is relevant to, or would be effective in protecting the population against natural or intentional biological threats. The emphasis on national defense in biomedical research results in profoundly different programs than those that would be based upon a public health and civic model. For instance, the focus of biodefense research on "one bug, one drug" strategies has become dominant at the expense of the development of broad-spectrum counter-measures which could be much more useful in situations like the current swine-flu pandemic. At the same time, funding has been cut for public health programs and local preparedness against potential natural or lab-generated outbreaks.

We need a stand down and a time out. We need a national moratorium on the opening of new biodefense facilities and, simultaneously, a serious and transparent reevaluation of the big picture. We need a great many more answers before our government pours yet more money into these programs and creates new public health risks and international strain.

Will the Concerns of Citizens Be Heard?

The concerns of citizens are easily drowned out or dismissed amid the many voices representing financial, academic and political interests. We offer the following recommendations in hopes that the perspective of the public will at last be heard in this new Congress and Administration. We do not attempt to address all aspects of biodefense policy, but focus specifically on the need to curb the proliferation of high containment bio-safety laboratories in our communities and to create a transparent, integrated system for federal oversight and regulation of research and development activities with select agents and other dangerous pathogens.

Periodical and Internet Sources Bibliography

The following articles have been selected to supplement the diverse views presented in this chapter.

Adam Cohen	"Should Medical Journals Print Info That Could Help Bioterrorists?," *Time*, December 27, 2011.
Laurie Garrett, interviewed by Brandon Keim	"How US Learned the Wrong Health Lessons from 9/11," *Wired*, September 9, 2011.
Karen Kaplan	"Burdens of Biodefense," *Nature*, May 19, 2010.
Lynn C. Klotz and Edward J. Sylvester	"Biohazard: Why US Bioterror Research Is More Dangerous Than Bioterrorism," *Foreign Policy*, October 13, 2009.
John Manuel	"Oversight Without Obstruction: The Challenge for High-Containment Labs," *Environmental Health Perspectives*, November 2008.
John Dudley Miller	"Postal Anthrax Aftermath: Has Biodefense Spending Made Us Safer?," *Scientific American*, November 2008.
Lynne Peeples	"Bioterrorism Funding Withers as Death Germs Thrive in Labs, Nature," *Huffington Post*, February 10, 2012.
Jesse Tucker	"Proliferation of Biodefense Laboratories and the Need for National Biosecurity," *Homeland Security Affairs*, 2008.
Beth Willis	"The Lab in My Backyard," *GeneWatch*, March–April 2010.
David Willman	"Inside Our Own Labs, the Threat of Another Anthrax Attack," *Washington Post*, June 10, 2011.

CHAPTER 3

How Should the United States Prepare for and Protect Against Bioterrorism?

Chapter Preface

Operated by the Centers for Disease Control and Prevention (CDC) and Department of Homeland Security (DHS), the Strategic National Stockpile (SNS) is a repository of countermeasures and supplies—including antibiotics, antitoxins, and vaccines—to support and replenish state and local health agencies in a national emergency or bioterrorism attack. It was initially established by the CDC and Department of Health and Human Services (HHS) as the National Pharmaceutical Stockpile (NPS) in 1999, effectively becoming the SNS in 2003 under the Homeland Security Act.

The SNS features a "Push Package" system intended to provide rapid and versatile delivery of countermeasures at the beginning of the event when the agent or toxin is undetermined. "These Push Packages are positioned in strategically located, secure warehouses ready for immediate deployment to a designated site within twelve hours of the federal decision to deploy SNS assets," states the CDC. Furthermore, if more supplies are necessary, vendor-managed inventory (VMI)—in which a vendor maintains the inventory of the supplier—can be delivered from twenty-four to thirty-six hours. Specialized VMI can also be deployed as a first response if the agent or toxin has been determined.

Some question, however, if the SNS has the United States adequately prepared for bioterrorism. "I'm sad to say that the language outlining the Strategic National Stockpile lends itself to a totally unwarranted sense that the federal government will back up hospitals, medical centers, surgical centers, and outpatient clinics during disasters," declares James M. Rush, an emergency-management expert who acted as the first logistics manager of the NPS. According to Rush, the supply of countermeasures are inadequately detailed, leaving health agencies in the dark: "The federal government should clearly state which categories of supplies, equipment, and pharmaceuticals will and will not be available to healthcare organizations and when and for how long healthcare organizations can count on Federal support."

In the following chapter, authors examine the United States' readiness for bioterrorism.

*"Local officials say simply planning the
exercise helped them prepare for a real
disaster, forcing coordination among
police, fire, public health, pharmacists
and others."*

Cities Ready with Mock
Bioterror Drills

Laura Meckler

*The following viewpoint discusses how the United States has
strengthened its preparedness for bioterrorism attacks with mock
bioterror drills. Simply planning mock bioterror drills has helped
increase coordination among the police, fire team, and the public,
according to the author. Although these bioterror drills help prepare the United States against an attack, it is argued that if the
drills aren't challenging enough, it could offer a false sense of security. Laura Meckler is a writer for the Associated Press.*

As you read, consider the following questions:

1. How long was the bioterror drill that took place in
   Tucson?
2. What one state is ready to receive the federal stockpile of
   drugs needed in a disaster?

3. According to the article, do these drills succeed in identifying weaknesses in the system?

Jeanne Williquett is playing her part well in a bioterrorism drama meant to test this city's readiness for an attack. She desperately tells anyone who will listen that she has anthrax.

"I have a fever," she tells a nurse, who nods along, trying to calm her. "They say anthrax starts with a fever."

Volunteers like Williquett, a hospice nurse, are helping local planners test Tucson's ability to quickly distribute antibiotics to a large number of people in response to a bioterrorist attack.

It's the sort of exercise other states and cities are likely to run as they work to upgrade and test their response systems. The federal government already has handed out $1 billion to help states plan for bioterrorism, with more on the way, and states are required to show they are making progress.

Just this month, federal officials conducted their own bioterrorism war game at the White House, playing out their response to a hypothetical international smallpox attack.

In Tucson, the three-day drill in November illustrated both the power and limitations of bioterrorism planning. Real nurses worked to calm Williquett and deal with other crises. But those in charge knew even before the test began exactly how the disaster was to unfold and just how they would handle it.

Local officials say simply planning the exercise helped them prepare for a real disaster, forcing coordination among police, fire, public health, pharmacists and others.

"When the big event happens you have to know the person on the other end of that line is someone you can trust and is going to do the job," said Les Caid, a battalion chief for the Tucson Fire Department, a chief organizer.

But outside experts caution that if exercises aren't challenging enough, they can offer a false sense of security.

In Tuscon, local planners are ahead of much of the nation, but it isn't clear whether the exercise actually tested their readiness for the worst.

Nationally, there is much work to be done.

Just one state, Florida, is ready to receive the federal stockpile of drugs and medical supplies needed in a disaster, according to a federal assessment this fall, although other states may have improved since then.

At the same time, many communities have little clue how they would handle a surge of injured patients or produce enough isolation beds to keep a crush of infectious people away from others.

A slew of new hires in public health, upgraded computer systems, detailed planning and drills like Tucson's are aimed at helping communities move ahead.

Bioterrorism planners from around the country came to watch Tucson's drill, looking for ideas.

"If something were to happen now, everyone has plans in place," said Vernon Jones, lead coordinator for the Fresco, Calif., Metropolitan Medical Response System. But independent plans developed by various local agencies aren't integrated, he said.

Jones plans to develop plans to deliver mass smallpox vaccinations and conduct a drill. Asked if he could vaccinate the 600,000 people in his community within a few days of an attack, he said bluntly: "No, nobody can."

In Montgomery County, Md., officials staged an exercise this fall that county police Capt. Mike Collins said identified several problems: Hospitals couldn't reach the public health department because someone had turned off the telephone ringer, and while they identified needed medical supplies, they didn't know how to get them.

In rural Graham County, Ariz., bioterrorism coordinator Dolores Herrera says the preparations are overwhelming. "It's so vague," she said. "Everything is a concept."

She said the county does not yet have a plan to dispense medicine in a mass attack.

Being in an isolated rural county two hours northeast of Tucson makes preparation particularly challenging, she said. "You only have so many nurses, so many doctors, so many pharmacists." And county officials have contacts but "no solid relationships" on Indian reservations.

The Tucson drill begins on a Wednesday when two men wielding fire extinguishers spray white gas representing anthrax spores onto a luncheon crowd.

Officials confirm that it's anthrax, and Arizona's governor immediately calls the federal Centers for Disease Control and Prevention in Atlanta to request backup medical supplies. The CDC's National Pharmaceutical Stockpile has 50-ton mobile pharmacies located at 12 different sites around the country. These "push packs," which contain antibiotics, vaccines and medical supplies, can be delivered to any town in America inside 12 hours.

Early Thursday, a smaller version with pretend medicines arrives at an Arizona Air National Guard hanger.

On Friday, hundreds of volunteers get descriptions of the characters they are to play, including medical histories and information about whether they were at the conference center when the anthrax was released.

Those who were there fill out medical forms and watch video tapes explaining basic facts about anthrax and the antibiotics. Pharmacists, including some brought out of retirement, answer questions and hand out drugs.

There's no way to know who inhaled the anthrax spores, so anyone at the conference center during the attack will be given antibiotics, just in case.

The system works: By the end of the day, antibiotics are distributed to nearly 2,000 people.

Throughout the day, workers are tested by volunteers who portray patients with particular medical problems or severe anxiety.

Take Annette Flannery, who refuses to accept that there is no way to diagnose exposure to anthrax.

"There has to be a test," she tells counselors. "You can't just be giving people medicine for no reason!"

Unable to convince her otherwise, counselors relent, telling her to see her own doctor on Monday for an anthrax test—where she'll be told again that one doesn't exist.

Williquett, 71, is also terrified. She is sure she has anthrax and is directed to a triage tent for immediate care.

"Anthrax doesn't sterilize you, does it?" Williquett asks a nurse, Carmen Diaz. "How long does it take for the antibiotics to work? Who pays for all of this? I don't have a lot of money."

Diaz answers all her questions—anthrax doesn't sterilize you, the antibiotics are free and should work right away—and sends her to the hospital for further evaluation and treatment.

The drill succeeds in identifying at least a few holes in the system.

The push pack of medicines was driven to Arizona from neighboring New Mexico, and local officials were at the state line to meet it. But the truck driver was operating on Eastern Standard Time while the people waiting were on Mountain Time. They didn't have a cell phone number to reach the driver.

At the convention center, the instructional videos played so softly that they were inaudible to anyone more than a foot from the TV.

And in the midst of placing orders from the pharmaceutical stockpile, the phone lines went down.

"Retired Air Force Col Randy Larsen, the commission's executive director, said the poor preparation for the swine flu epidemic in 2009 was proof that the country was not positioned to respond to something more serious."

US Not Ready for Bioterrorist Attack: Report

Daily Times

In the following viewpoint, the Daily Times *argues that the United States has not made progress against the increasing threat of bioterrorism. The Commission on the Prevention of Weapons of Mass Destruction Proliferation gave President Barack Obama's administration a failing grade for its attempt to prepare for a bioterrorist attack. The viewpoint argues that each of the last three administrations have been slow to respond to and recognize a biological threat. The* Daily Times *is an English language Pakistani newspaper.*

As you read, consider the following questions:

1. What urgent threats does Bob Graham claim the United States is failing to address?

2. Why does Randy Larsen mention the shortage of the H1N1 vaccine?
3. What five steps did the report recommend the United States should take in order to protect against bioterrorism threats?

The US is not prepared for a biological terrorist attack, said a congressionally mandated panel in a report released on Tuesday.

The Commission on the Prevention of Weapons of Mass Destruction Proliferation gave President Barack Obama's administration a failing grade for its efforts to prepare for and respond to a biological attack, such as the release of deadly viruses or bacteria.

"Nearly a decade after September 11, 2001 . . . and one month after the Christmas Day bombing attempt, the US is failing to address several urgent threats, especially bioterrorism," said former senator Bob Graham, chairman of the commission. "Each of the last three administrations has been slow to recognise and respond to the biothreat. But we no longer have the luxury of a slow learning curve, when we know Al Qaeda is interested in bioweapons."

He was referring to an attempted bombing on a US airliner on Christmas Day. A Nigerian man, Umar Farouk Abdulmutallab, is accused of trying to ignite an explosive aboard an airliner as it was nearing its destination, Detroit.

Retired Air Force Col Randy Larsen, the commission's executive director, said the poor preparation for the swine flu epidemic in 2009 was proof that the country was not positioned to respond to something more serious. Larsen pointed to the early shortage of H1N1 vaccine despite a six-month warning from health officials that the disease would be potentially deadly. He said nobody in the Obama administration had taken the lead on protecting the country against bioterrorism.

"Especially troubling is the lack of priority given to the development of medical countermeasures—the vaccines and medicines that would be required to mitigate the consequences of an attack," said the report.

The report recommended five steps the government should take to deal with the threat of bioterrorism: a comprehensive review of the domestic programme to secure dangerous pathogens, the development of a national strategy to advance the ability to conduct forensic analyses of bioterror attacks, tightened government oversight of laboratories that deal with dangerous pathogens, promotion of a culture of security awareness among scientists, and expansion of the country's rapid response plan to prevent biological attacks from inflicting mass casualties.

The commission was formed by Congress to evaluate the government's readiness for a terror attack involving weapons of mass destruction. Its report follows a study released on Monday that warned that Al Qaeda is still pursuing technology to conduct a biological, chemical or even nuclear attack against the US.

| *"The odds are impossible to gauge, but there is no question we're vulnerable."*

Mass Vaccination Could Be Necessary to Protect Against Smallpox

Newsweek

In the following viewpoint, Newsweek argues that mass vaccination would save lives in a large-scale smallpox attack. The odds of such an attack are impossible to gauge, the article says, but the United States is at risk. Due to the urging of the Centers for Disease Control and Prevention, state governments are now devising plans in which they will vaccinate the masses in case of a smallpox attack. The article argues that it is better to be prepared in such an event than to deal with the alternative.

As you read, consider the following questions:

1. In what year did the United States abandon routine smallpox vaccinations?
2. What is the incubation period of the smallpox virus?
3. What major event do the authors discuss to demonstrate that emergencies can defy carefully laid prevention plans?

The United States abandoned routine smallpox vaccination in 1972, and never regretted the decision. No one on earth has contracted natural smallpox since 1977. The World Health Organization declared the disease "eradicated" in 1980, and no country has vaccinated children since 1984. Unfortunately the variola virus, which causes smallpox, is still very much alive. The Soviet government cultivated a huge stockpile for military use during the 1980s, in violation of international law. The stockpile was eventually destroyed, and today the only acknowledged variola samples are held in government laboratories in the United States and Russia. But the Soviet stockpile has never been fully accounted for. And recent events—the World Trade Center attack, the anthrax attacks, the persistence of Al Qaeda and the mounting hostilities with Saddam Hussein—have lent new urgency to an old question. Could terrorists hit us with smallpox?

United States Vulnerable

The odds are impossible to gauge, but there is no question we're vulnerable. Even as they called for an end to routine vaccination, Millar and Lane warned that the loss of widespread immunity would "raise our susceptibility to smallpox as a weapon of biologic warfare." Those of us vaccinated before 1972 may still have some residual protection, but the 119 million Americans born since then are about as defenseless as the ones who greeted Columbus 500 years ago. "Although smallpox has long been feared as the most devastating of all infectious diseases," the Johns Hopkins-based Working Group on Civilian Biodefense has written, "its potential for devastation today is far greater than at any previous time."

Federal officials are as concerned as anyone else, and the Bush administration has made "biosecurity" a high priority. Two weeks ago the federal government came forward with a blueprint for quickly vaccinating the whole country in the event of a smallpox attack. And Health and Human Services Secretary Tommy Thompson has presented the White House with a plan that could lead to routine "pre-attack" vaccination of up to 10 million health and emergency workers—and perhaps even private citizens—by early 2004. The HHS plan doesn't have a precise timetable, but it includes three phases. To start, the government would vaccinate the 500,000 health workers most likely to encounter patients during an outbreak. Later, as new vaccine stocks are developed and licensed by the Food and Drug Administration, other—emergency workers would become eligible. And once that has happened, private citizens would gain voluntary access. The proposal is not yet policy, just an option that the president will mull as he contemplates his next move in the "war on terror." Last week members of the team that crafted it spoke at length to NEWSWEEK about its origins and evolution, and the prospects for keeping America safe from smallpox. Their mood was summed up by Tom Ridge, director of the Office of Homeland Security. "You have people in this world who hate America and who have said they will use any means to harm us," he said. "You have to be prepared." . . .

At the urging of the federal Centers for Disease Control and Prevention, state and local governments are now devising plans to vaccinate everyone during a smallpox attack. Health workers would still track and vaccinate the contacts of known victims. But under the new plan, laid out in a 48-page "Smallpox Vaccination Clinic Guide," states and cities must also establish clinics that can open quickly during an emergency to screen, counsel and vaccinate anyone who walks through the door. The CDC guide includes blueprints for model clinics in which staffs of 117 workers can vaccinate nearly 3,000 people during each eight-hour shift. Most experts agree that if health departments can pull off what the Feds have in mind, the mass-vaccination strategy will save lives. Smallpox doesn't spread easily from person to person during its seven- to 17-day incubation period, and even infected people can often avoid serious illness if they're vaccinated within four days. Inoculating the nation that quickly would pose enormous challenges, says Kaplan, "but it's not impossible at all." . . .

Being Prepared for Emergencies

While stockpiling the old vaccines for emergencies, the government has also ordered up 210 million doses of a second-generation vaccine grown in cell cultures rather than cow pustules. That vaccine, developed by Acambis of Cambridge, England, will contain the same virus as the older ones and carry most of the same risks, but it will be less likely to harbor impurities. HHS expects to have 70 million doses on hand by the end of the year. Meanwhile, no one is sweating over a shortage of vaccine. "In an emergency," says Dr. Anthony Fauci of the National Institute of Allergy and Infectious Diseases, "we'd have enough to vaccinate everybody tomorrow."

Being prepared surely beats the alternative. But emergencies have a way of defying carefully laid plans. Just think back to last year's anthrax scare, says Neal Cohen, a former New York City health commissioner who now heads a preparedness group called the Center on Bioterrorism. Experts predicted confidently that postal workers wouldn't be infected by sealed mail—until they were. And they dismissed the possibility that one tainted letter could contaminate others—until it happened. "A lot of our assumptions turned out to be faulty," he says. "We learned how little we really understood about the risks." Could freeway traffic stall response plans in L.A. or Atlanta? What about airport closures? And suppose terrorists managed to combine a smallpox release with a September 11-style assault that placed competing demands on the response system? "If there's more than one form of attack," says Millar, the virus hunter, "the task of vaccinating everyone in the country in a week becomes mind-boggling." ...

If someone could quantify the threat of a smallpox attack, this debate would be winnable. We could weigh the vaccine's hazards against those of an outbreak, and declare one set of hazards more serious. Without that intelligence, it would be hard to justify a peacetime vaccination drive. But nobody is planning one. The new HHS plan recognizes the need for a well-immunized emergency-response network, but it doesn't propose a return to compulsory childhood smallpox shots. It simply envisions letting people choose their own risks. "We'd set it up on a voluntary basis," says Thompson, "and if you wanted it you could have it." Would the risk be worth taking? Maybe not. But as Bicknell points out, most of us face higher risks every day without thinking twice.

It would be nice, of course, if we could have the immunity without the risk. That may soon be possible. The government is stocking up on vaccinia immune globulin, a medicine that can ease adverse reactions to the smallpox vaccines, and funding research to develop entirely new ways of immunizing people. The most promising of the third-generation vaccines—based on a weakened vaccinia strain known as MVA (Modified Vaccinia Ankara)—is already being used in gene therapy and AIDS-vaccine experiments, and even extremely ill patients seem to tolerate it well. After reconfirming MVA's safety, says Fauci, researchers will begin testing its efficacy against smallpox. At the least, he says, it may provide a good booster for people vaccinated decades earlier. When scientists devise a vaccine that is as safe as MVA and as effective as Dryvax, perhaps we'll all take the shot and stop worrying about how to vaccinate the population in 10 days flat. Short of that, no plan can keep us completely immune from danger.

| "In our opinion, pre-vaccination of the
population at large is unnecessary."

Mass Vaccination Is Not Necessary to Protect Against Smallpox

Fred Hutchinson Cancer Research Center

In the following viewpoint, the Fred Hutchinson Cancer Research Center claims mass vaccination would be unnecessary to contain a large-scale smallpox attack. According to a study by the Hutchinson Center, surveillance and containment—the quarantine of infected individuals and immunization of their immediate contacts— would sufficiently prevent the spread of the smallpox. The researchers found that prevaccination of the public would slightly lower the number of fatalities, but the vaccine's rate of serious illness and deaths would counter the additional lives saved. The Fred Hutchinson Cancer Research Center is a leading cancer research institute.

As you read, consider the following questions:

1. In what timeframe would surveillance and containment be most effective, as described in the viewpoint?
2. As cited in the viewpoint, what are the probabilities of

Fred Hutchinson Cancer Research Center, "Mass Vaccination Unnecessary in the Event of a Large Bioterrorist US Smallpox Attack," October 16, 2006. Copyright © 2006 by Fred Hutchinson Cancer Research Center. All rights reserved. Reproduced by permission.

severe illness and death from the smallpox vaccine?

3. Where are the two laboratories where the smallpox virus still exists?

Mass vaccination would not be necessary in the event of a large-scale smallpox bioterrorist attack in the United States, according to a study led by researchers at Fred Hutchinson Cancer Research Center that appears online in the *International Journal of Infectious Diseases*.

Instead, the current U.S. government policy of post-release surveillance, prompt containment of victims and vaccination of hospital workers and close contacts would be sufficient to thwart an epidemic, according to lead author Ira M. Longini Jr., Ph.D., a world leader in using mathematical and statistical methods to study the natural diseases.

"We found that a well-prepared response of surveillance and containment, if done quickly, within a day or two of detecting the first smallpox case, would contain a large attack if up to 500 people were infected," said Longini, a member of the Public Health Sciences Division at the Hutchinson Center and a professor of biostatistics at the University of Washington School of Public Health and Community Medicine. These results apply to scenarios involving even the most virulent, fatal forms of the virus.

However, Longini emphasizes, failure to quickly isolate known smallpox cases and vaccinate their close contacts could thwart the containment of an epidemic.

These findings emerge from a committee of smallpox experts—including infectious-disease modelers, epidemiologists, statisticians and clinicians—who were commissioned by former Secretary of Health and Human Services Tommy Thompson to evaluate a variety of intervention strategies to determine whether the United States could contain a large-scale smallpox bioterrorist attack and, if so, how.

Settling the Issues of Smallpox Containment

Specifically, the researchers were charged with determining whether surveillance and containment—isolation of detected smallpox cases and vaccination of their close contacts—would be sufficient to contain a large attack. They also wanted to find out whether other interventions, such as mass pre-vaccination of the general public, pre-vaccination of hospital personnel, vaccination of the target community and closure of schools after a smallpox release would help contain the spread of the disease.

Thompson's senior science adviser, Donald Ainslie (D.A.) Henderson, the physician and epidemiologist who oversaw the World Health Organization's successful campaign to eradicate smallpox from the world in the late 1970s, served as a consultant to the committee, known as the Smallpox Modeling Working Group. The group was convened by the Secretary's Advisory Council on Public Health Preparedness, a branch of the U.S. Department of Health and Human Services.

"Earlier studies recommended mass pre-vaccination of the general population to protect against a smallpox attack. None of us on the committee believed this was necessary, including D.A. Henderson, who intimately understands the natural history of the virus," Longini said. "The secretary of Health and Human Services wanted to settle such issues regarding smallpox containment once and for all, and this was our charge."

While the researchers did find that mass vaccination would slightly reduce the number of deaths from smallpox, they also found that the rate of severe illness and death caused by the vaccine itself would cancel out any benefit from mass vaccination. One person in 10,000 will have a severe reaction and one in a million will die from the vaccine, Longini said.

"Precautionary vaccination of hospital personnel and post-release vaccination of the target population would further contain the spread of smallpox, but at a cost of many more people being vaccinated," said co-author and Hutchinson Center biostatistician M. Elizabeth (Betz) Halloran, M.D., D.Sc. "The financial cost and potential illness and death related to vaccination must be weighed against the potential benefits in the event of an attack. In our opinion, pre-vaccination of the population at large is unnecessary," she said. Longini, Halloran and colleagues also found that closure of schools after a smallpox attack would have a minimal effect in preventing transmission of the disease, and that any delay in quarantining infected individuals would take a much greater toll on the community than failing to pre-vaccinate potential cases.

Taking Real-World Unpredictability into Account

To conduct the study, Longini and colleagues created a computer model that calculated the spread of smallpox via aerosol dissemination—the most likely choice of terrorists—within a community of 50,000. Members of this virtual community interacted the way people normally do: within households, neighborhoods, preschool groups, schools, a community hospital and the community at large. The age distribution and household sizes were based on the U.S. census for 2000.

Predicting the spread of an infectious disease such as smallpox requires much more than simply connecting dots on a map. Instead Longini and colleagues rely on a tool called stochastic modeling to take into account real-world unpredictability, as well as many factors about the disease and the affected population. In constructing these models, Longini and colleagues begin with assumptions about how people interact and how the virus spreads. They also introduce and evaluate the effectiveness of various intervention strategies.

The study represents the first attempt to integrate what science knows about the natural history of smallpox—how various forms of the disease manifest over time—with human patterns of behavior to construct the most-comprehensive model of a smallpox epidemic to date.

Possible Side Effects to Smallpox Vaccinations © 2002 Signe Wilkinson. Used with the permission of Signe Wilkinson and the Cartoonist Group.

"If smallpox appeared in Seattle tomorrow, which it could do, I'm absolutely confident that we could contain it if our recommendations for surveillance and containment were put into practice. I rest easier now that we've done this study," Longini said. "The process was kind of like unveiling the enemy to the point where we really understood it. This research has helped us demystify the threat a bit."

Although smallpox has been eliminated as a naturally-occurring disease, the virus still exists in two approved laboratories in the United States and Russia. The Centers for Disease Control and Prevention classifies it as a "Category A" agent, presenting the greatest potential threat for harming public health if developed and used as a bioterrorist agent.

The Variola Virus

Smallpox is caused by the variola virus, which emerged thousands of years ago. Variola major, the most common form of the virus, is divided into four subcategories: ordinary (which accounts for about 90 percent of cases and has a fatality rate of about 30 percent), modified (which occurs in people who have been vaccinated and has a death rate of about 10 percent), and flat and hemorrhagic (both very rare and uniformly fatal).

According to the CDC, exposure to the variola virus is followed by an incubation period of seven to 17 days, during which people are not contagious and feel fine. The first symptoms emerge during what is called the prodrome phase, and they include head and body aches, fatigue, a high fever and, sometimes, vomiting. This phase lasts two to four days and at this point people may or may not be contagious. Then a rash emerges all over the body and grows increasingly severe over the next 20 or so days, eventually forming scabs; during this period people are contagious, particularly during the first seven to 10 days of the rash. The disease eventually resolves and contagion ends after all of the scabs have fallen off. People who survive are then considered to be immune from smallpox.

A person can become infected by prolonged, face-to-face exposure with someone who is contagious, direct contact with infected bodily fluids or a contaminated object, such as bedding or clothing, and exposure to an aerosol release.

Routine smallpox vaccination ended in 1972, which leaves at least 43 percent of the U.S. population unvaccinated, Longini said. Research suggests that those previously vaccinated may still have substantial residual immunity although, if infected, they could still transmit the virus to others. Those most vulnerable to the virus are the very young and those whose immune systems are compromised due to HIV/AIDS, cancer or some other medical condition. An estimated 50 million Americans fall into this category, Longini said.

> *"In current bioterror response plans, it often seems as though the actions and concerns of laypeople are . . . problems to be controlled."*

Citizens Must Be Prepared to Respond to Bioterrorism

Richard J. Danzig, Rachel Kleinfeld, and Philipp C. Bleek

In the following viewpoint, Richard J. Danzig, Rachel Kleinfeld, and Philipp C. Bleek argue that bioterrorism planning ignores citizens' involvement in their own security and makes assumptions about the capacities of professionals and emergency responders. However, the authors state, citizen preparedness is critical for several reasons: Professionals alone will not be able to cope with large-scale attacks, laypeople will be the first to respond to emergencies as well as provide supplies and services, and citizen preparedness will ensure psychological and political well-being. Danzig is chairman of the Center for a New American Security, Kleinfeld is cofounder and chief executive officer of the Truman National Security Project, and Bleek is an assistant professor at the Monterey Institute of International Studies.

As you read, consider the following questions:

1. Who are the "worried well" and what is their impact?
2. In what ways does predominant bioterrorism planning view laypeople as problems, according to the authors?
3. What would be the role of nearby laypeople to help a person showing symptoms of a bioterror-related illness, as detailed by the authors?

For most issues of personal safety, responsibility is implicitly shared between the public and the government. Individuals are expected to wear bicycle helmets, refrain from smoking in bed, cross at crosswalks, and take other everyday safety measures, while the government takes responsibility for enforcing traffic regulations, checking on building code violations, funding fire departments, and deploying police. Yet national security—protecting the country against enemies—is viewed both by our government and our public as almost exclusively government's responsibility. The public is implicitly regarded as a vulnerable, dependent population to be protected by the government; in this context, members of the public are not treated as co-equals in ensuring their own personal safety.

These differences are reflected in the different response paradigms for handling the twin threats of pandemic influenza and bioterrorism. While pandemic influenza planning assumes the need for layperson education and action to contain the spread of disease and reduce risks and consequences, present preparations for bioterrorism follow a professional paradigm with little consideration as to how laypeople could be involved in their own security.

Assumptions of Bioterrorism Planners

In the present paradigm bioterrorism planners at the federal, state, and local levels tend to assume that:

- Rapid awareness of an attack will be achieved by either environmental sensors or health surveillance systems.

These systems will create an alarm that will trigger federal-state coordination through an "Emergency Management Assistance Compact."

- Political leaders and professionals, principally including public health officials and medical personnel, will inform the public about what is occurring, and will direct them to appropriate professional resources.

- The public health sector (assisted, if deemed necessary, by first responders such as emergency medical personnel, firemen, policemen, and the National Guard) will create Points of Distribution (PODs) at which they will distribute drugs or vaccines that will counter the pathogen that has been employed.

- Hospitals will treat those who are not protected by drugs and vaccines. Insofar as hospital capacities are overwhelmed, alternate care sites, including private sector facilities such as hotels and college dormitories, will be used to inspect and treat casualties. As required, medical personnel from other areas will supplement local resources.

- Hospitals and alternative sites will have to cope with perhaps ten times the number of those who are actually infected because the "worried well"—those who fear they have been infected but have not been will demand treatment. These worried well will burden the medical system.

Most experts would describe these challenges as Herculean but nonetheless predictable in the wake of a mass aerosol attack. If the United States could meet these challenges, most policy experts believe we would be reasonably well prepared. As a result, we now invest approximately $5 billion per year in these efforts, devoting the bulk of our funding and planning resources to alarm systems, first responder capabilities, drug development, creation of stockpiles and distribution systems, amplification of surge capacity in hospitals, and (to a limited extent) the preparation and communication of messages from authorities to residents in affected areas so as to calm them and reduce the number of worried well.

This response paradigm considers only what professionals must do to care for the public after a bioterror attack. Professionals will discover an attack, then group, route, and organize laypeople into the appropriate categories for response. Professionals will treat individuals as needed, based on professionally determined triage. Professionals will provide accurate and timely information to the public.

A Problem, Not a Resource

The predominant planning paradigm therefore considers layperson response as one of a number of post-attack problems, not as a resource. Laypeople are seen, at best, as subjects for control, at worst, obstacles that reduce survival rates and impede recovery operations through ill-informed or self-interested behavior. Many professionals fear "scaring" laypeople by sharing the burden of safety. It is common for professionals in many arenas, from flight attendants to event managers, to treat those under their care as impediments to the seamless implementation of standard operating procedures. If people would do what they were told, go where they were sent, and follow directions, the jobs of professionals would be far easier. In current bioterror response plans, it often seems as though the actions and concerns of laypeople are akin to the pathogens that have been released: they are problems to be controlled.

None of these premises are squarely wrong and none of these priorities are irrational. But taken together they yield a program that will fail in the face of catastrophic attack. Our current bioterror strategy is analogous to training firefighters in new techniques, increasing our supply of volunteer firemen, and purchasing improved equipment for firehouses, while neglecting to preposition fire extinguishers, run fire drills to teach evacuation plans, or instruct people to evacuate by stairs rather than elevators. It addresses only half of the problem—and in doing so, creates a much more difficult task for professionals.

To correct the failures of the professional paradigm, those engaged on this issue must not only ask what professionals and bureaucracies need to better prepare for a catastrophic bioterror attack but also what the public will experience and expect after an attack. What can laypeople do to protect themselves, their loved ones, and their communities, reduce their own casualties, and otherwise meet their own expectations? What does the government need to do to empower laypeople, to help them take care of themselves and reduce the demands on and expectations of government? Adopting this perspective makes laypeople potential assets as well as potential problems.

Four Compelling Reasons to Prepare Laypeople

Four compelling reasons support this approach. First, the skills of citizens will be demanded because professionals will not be sufficiently numerous to cope with mass aerosol biological attacks on their own. As illustrated below, America's best-laid plans for building surge capacity in hospitals and related facilities still leave our emergency health systems well behind the likely demand. While enhancing the supply of professional capability is essential, it is also difficult, expensive, slow, and yields only marginal gains. Complementing a professional, supply-enhancement strategy with an equally robust demand-reduction strategy is likely to yield greater protection at less cost.

Second, even if policymakers do not plan for layperson care, it will occur. Laypeople are often the first to respond to an emergency. Friends, family, and co-workers are the most likely to be nearby when a person exhibits symptoms associated with a bioterror-related illness, and laypeople will generally play the key role in deciding when and how to seek medical attention, where to go, and how to support treatment. The most reasonable planning premise is that in the wake of a mass attack, ordinary men

Communication: A Central Feature

Bioterrorism can result in widespread fear, outrage, and elevated risk perceptions, resulting in intense pressure on government officials to "do something." Poor communication can result in at-risk populations overreacting, taking inappropriate actions, and losing trust in government officials or agencies. . . . A future bioterrorist event would inevitably require state and local agencies to communicate with multiple and diverse audiences. Communication must be a central feature of responding to a bioterrorism event.

Communication in such events serves multiple purposes, including informing and instructing widely diverse audiences, minimizing fear and anxiety, encouraging individuals to adopt appropriate protective actions, building trust, and minimizing or dispelling misinformation or rumors. Addressing the unique information and communication needs of special population groups can help public officials to select the appropriate strategies and develop the right messages for specific audiences.

Marty McGough, Loreeta Leer Frank, Stacia Tipton, Tim L. Tinker, and Elaine Vaughan, "Communicating the Risks of Bioterrorism and other Emergencies in a Diverse Society: A Case Study of Special Populations in North Dakota," Biosecurity and Bioterrorism: Biodefense Strategy, Practice, and Science, *vol. 3, no. 3, 2005.*

and women will provide health care (or advice on seeking health care) to loved ones, particularly in the short term. If movement is restricted because of contamination (a probability in the wake of an anthrax attack) or contagion (a certainty in the wake of a smallpox attack), lay capabilities are even more likely to be the only resource immediately present in circumstances of need. The United States can either plan for the eventuality of layperson-supplied health care or fail to prepare and have it occur anyway without assistance or planning.

Third, even if professionals were able to meet America's post-attack healthcare needs, laypeople would be essential in other ways. Unless and until the military is mobilized and deployed, it is ordinary individuals, not "first responders," health care professionals, or microbiologists who will need to provide the power, food, water, sanitation, burial, transport, mass communications, and other supplies and services that will sustain our society in the face of bioterrorist attacks. These ordinary people will be de facto "first suppliers," and must understand the needs and threats that they face, be reasonably capable of caring for themselves and their families, and be well informed about how they should do their jobs without unduly endangering themselves.

Finally, beyond these practical needs, there are compelling political and psychological reasons for adopting a layperson-centric perspective. Catastrophic attacks on America can have tactical ends—to kill or maim, to cripple our economy, to distract our military, to damage our image, to galvanize foreign constituencies—and strengthening lay response systems can help to counter these ambitions. But first and foremost, these attacks will pose a strategic political and psychological challenge. Terrorists seek to reduce confidence in government; their attacks sow fear to weaken public resolve. It is in the minds of our citizens that an attack's success or failure will be determined. As [author] Danzig has previously written:

> A much quoted insight of [German military theorist Carl von] Clausewitz is as applicable to terrorism as to conventional conflicts. "Psychological forces exert a decisive influence on the elements involved in war." A catastrophic attack will be a psychological and a political intensifier: it will either increase

our national unity and support of our government or, as terrorists intend, it will induce divisiveness, loss of confidence, and distraction.

A public that is unprepared for attack, and that is unable to take positive actions that enable self-protection, is far more vulnerable psychologically as well as physically. If laypeople can be made aware of the threat, have the time to absorb and normalize the idea, and be provided with actions they can undertake to protect themselves, they will be far more resilient. If, concomitantly, expectations about government care are lowered to realistic levels, the polity will be less beset with recriminations and broken confidences.

Uniting the Population

For us there is no more critical question about the response to bioterrorism than this: In the wake of these attacks, does our population unite, increase its confidence in and support for our government, retrieve its sense of security, and redouble its sense of purpose, or does our population divide, lose confidence, and become diverted by problems ensuing from attacks, thus diminishing our ability to pursue our previous political and military agenda?

The latter is not only bad in its own right; it will also encourage more attacks. Improvement in this political and psychological dimension is not, then, just a matter of consequence management. Our failures and achievements in addressing the concerns of our citizens and helping them to help themselves will go a long way to determining whether attacks will be defeated and therefore whether future attacks will be encouraged or deterred.

As [German philosopher] Friedrich Nietzsche said, "Forgetting our objectives is the most frequent stupidity in which we indulge ourselves." Our objective in the face of a bioterror attack is not to increase surge capacity, improve sensor alerts, or make distribution systems more efficient—important as these tactics will be. Our larger aims are to minimize injury, death, and economic destruction. Beyond this, our greatest goal is to maximize societal resilience so that America will not be fundamentally destroyed or degraded by terror. A knowledgeable and empowered public, which is able to take responsibility for itself and to lower its expectations on the government to realistic levels, is imperative to achieving these goals. That requires implementing the kind of public preparedness and empowerment that the *National Strategy for Combating Terrorism* contents itself with only reciting. To instantiate this ideal, we begin by asking: What will the public expect and require as support in the wake of a major bioterrorist attack? Put another way, we take up the challenge that the United Kingdom Parliamentary Report on Britain's July 2005 terror attacks identified as central:

> There is an overarching, fundamental lesson to be learnt . . . emergency plans should be re-cast from the point of view of people involved in a major or catastrophic incident, rather than focusing primarily on the point of view of each emergency service. A change of mindset is needed to bring about the necessary shift in focus, from incidents to individuals, and from processes to people.

Periodical and Internet Sources Bibliography

The following articles have been selected to supplement the diverse views presented in this chapter.

David C. Ake	"Technology Only a Small Part of Detecting Bioterrorist Threats," *National Defense*, September 2011.
Rae Burke	"Preparedness for Bioterrorism," *GEN*, October 15, 2007.
Mark Harris and Kevin Yeskey	"Bioterrorism and the Vital Role of Family Physicians," *American Family Physician*, July 1, 2011.
Barry Kellman	"Heeding the Warning of Bioterrorism," BioPrepWatch.com, January 26, 2010.
Jim Kouri	"Report Card: Bioterrorism Preparedness Gets Thumbs Down by Bipartisan Group," Renewamerica.com, October 15, 2011.
Betsy McKay	"Verdict on Smallpox Cache Near," *Wall Street Journal*, May 16, 2011.
Edward P. Richards	"The United States Smallpox Bioterrorism Preparedness Plan: Rational Response or Potemkin Planning?," *William Mitchell Law Review*, vol. 36, 2010.
Steve Sternberg	"US Government Stockpiles New, Safer Smallpox Vaccine," *USA Today*, May 25, 2010.
Thomas F. Stinson, Jean Kinsey, Dennis Degeneffe, and Koel Ghosh	"Defending America's Food Supply Against Terrorism: Who Is Responsible? Who Should Pay?," *Choices*, First Quarter, 2007.

OPPOSING
VIEWPOINTS®
SERIES

CHAPTER 4

What Anti-Bioterrorism
Policies Should the
United States Have?

Chapter Preface

In August 2010, the US Department of Health and Human Services Secretary Kathleen Sebelius released an investigation of the federal government's bioterrorism and emergency response system, *The Public Health Emergency Medical Countermeasures Enterprise Review: Transforming the Enterprise to Meet Long-Range National Needs.* "Our nation must have a system that is nimble and flexible enough to produce medical countermeasures quickly in the face of any attack or threat, whether it's a threat we know about today or a new one," Sebelius claims. "By moving towards a 21st century countermeasures enterprise with a strong base of discovery, a clear regulatory pathway, and agile manufacturing, we will be able to respond faster and more effectively to public health threats."

The review cites challenges in the development of medical countermeasures (MCMs) under Project BioShield, which was enacted after the anthrax attacks of 2001. "Project BioShield provides funds to procure MCMs once they are reasonably far along in the development pipeline and provides the most visible assurance to industry about the government's intent to provide a market for these products," the review states, "however, filling the discovery and developmental pipeline with needed product candidates eligible for Project BioShield against important . . . agents has been slower and more costly than anticipated, as has been maintaining and sustaining the federal stockpile of MCMs." The review maintains that new, novel developments for the prevention and treatment of emerging viruses are not encouraged by the market or investments, and potential innovation "languishes in academic laboratories or small biotech companies."

As a result, a new strategy in key areas of the MCM enterprise is outlined in the review: improving innovation, science, and capacity on a regulatory level; enhancing domestic manufacturing capacities; aiding partners with development and manufacturing services; finding new ways to work with partners; boosting financial incentives; easing the path from concept to advanced development stages; and improving management and administration. "Finally, this review recognizes that fulfilling the goals of a successful MCM enterprise . . . ultimately rests on a strong public health system, which requires improved global and national surveillance, a trained workforce, and the infrastructure, including links to the health system, that enables delivery and administration of MCMs at the right time and to the right people."

The following chapter further examines the bioterrorism policies of the United States. Authors offer varying opinions on the effectiveness of the nation's current response systems and policies.

> *"Cutting funding from Project
> Bioshield limits America's ability to
> rapidly respond to bioterror events and
> pandemic outbreaks."*

Project Bioshield Is Necessary to Keep Americans Safe

Eric S. Morse

Project BioShield was enacted by the US Congress in response to the 2001 anthrax attacks, allocating about $5 billion to biodefense. Eric S. Morse declares in the following viewpoint that the program is a form of insurance against bioterrorism and opposes cutting its funds. He insists that Project Bioshield has enabled the US Department of Health and Human Services to conduct research and develop countermeasures to anthrax, botulism, smallpox, and swine flu. The threat of bioterrorism is real and increasing in likelihood, the author maintains, and Project BioShield ensures that the government is capable of performing in such an emergency. Morse is the managing editor of the National Strategy Forum Review *and a doctoral candidate in political science at Loyola University Chicago.*

As you read, consider the following questions:

1. How does Morse describe the preparedness of the United

Eric S. Morse, "Russian Roulette with Project Bioshield," *National Strategy Forum Review*, 2010. Copyright © 2010 by the National Strategy Forum. All rights reserved. Reproduced by permission.

States during the swine flu outbreak of 2009?

2. What two options are available to the public in the scenario of a major bioterrorist attack, as stated by Morse?

3. Why is the prospect of funding cuts to Project Bioshield ironic to the author in the context of recent healthcare reform?

The thing about Russian Roulette is that if you pull the trigger enough times, you will eventually end up on in a world of hurt. On July 2nd [2010], House Democrats, under the leadership of Congressman David Obey, D-WI, Chairman of the Appropriations Committee, proposed an appropriations bill that would strip $2 billion from the nation's bioterrorism emergency fund, Project BioShield, to pay for increases in other federal programs, including education. Under the House proposal, the Department of Health and Human Services (HHS) would be required to cut $2 billion from funds reserved for pandemic flu vaccines, private medical research, and counter-bioterrorism programs. [The funds were not cut.]

Congressional reports contend that terrorists are more likely to obtain and use a biological weapon of mass destruction than a nuclear weapon. These reports recommended that a national program be maintained that enhances response capabilities to prevent biological attacks from inflicting mass casualties.

The Project BioShield Act was passed in 2004 under the recommendation of President [George W.] Bush. BioShield's main provisions are to: 1) relax procedures for chemical, biological, radiological, and nuclear (CBRN) terrorism-related spending; 2) guarantee a federal government market for new CBRN medical countermeasures; and 3) permit emergency use of unapproved countermeasures. Also in 2004, the Department of Homeland Security Appropriations Act (P.L. 108-90) appropriated $5.593 billion to Project BioShield for fiscal years 2004–2013. Funds are typically used to purchase, store, and research medical countermeasures to respond to biological attacks or outbreaks.

These laws have allowed HHS to facilitate critical, expedited programs that prepare America for biological disasters. For example, under Project BioShield, HHS set aside $2.3 billion to acquire medical countermeasures against biological threats such as anthrax, botulism, radiation poisoning, and smallpox. Congress has also tapped into these resources to pay for medical countermeasures against biological threats. In 2009, for instance, the Omnibus Appropriations Act (P.L. 111-8) transferred $412 million to pay for countermeasures and advanced research and development against the Swine Flu outbreak. More recently, in 2010, President Obama has asked for a $305 million to support additional countermeasure advanced research, development, and purchase. To date, Project BioShield has purchased about $2 billion of biological countermeasures from the U.S. Strategic National Stockpile. Currently, there is less than $2.4 billion left in the BioShield purse.

Some commentators contend that the BioShield fund has not been spent wisely or effectively, and that the original objective has fallen short of expectations, particularly in the area of providing incentives to the private sector for research and development of countermeasures. Others see the BioShield as a necessary safety net for likely threat scenarios.

Senators Judd Gregg, Richard Burr and Joe Lieberman are in opposition to the funding redirection. These three senators, along with thirteen of their colleagues, sent a letter to Senate Majority Leader Harry Reid and Minority Leader Mitch McConnell asking for the amendment to be overturned, and stating that the BioShield fund should not be used as a "piggy bank" for other federal spending. Senator Gregg commented: "The Project BioShield rescission included in the House amendment, or any similar future rescission, would devastate the BioShield program by cutting a majority of the program's remaining funding, which is intended for the procurement of new vaccines and counter-

Financial Incentive

The federal government is frequently perceived by pharmaceutical and vaccine manufacturers as an uncertain and low-profit market and, as a result, large pharmaceutical companies have largely avoided the development of products for use by the government in defense against the biological threat agents, because the expected profits do not justify the opportunity costs. . . . Project BioShield was initiated in an attempt to provide a financial incentive to manufacturers to develop the products needed for defense against chemical, biological, radiological, and nuclear threats. The creation of the permanent special reserve fund reduced the level of uncertainty regarding the government market.

Philip K. Russell, "Project BioShield:
What It Is, Why It Is Needed, and Its
Accomplishments So Far," Clinical Infectious
Diseases, vol. 45, Supplement 1, 2007.

measures. It is critically important that we make sure these potentially lifesaving funds are used for their intended purposes and not used as a convenient political offset for more new spending."

A Form of Bioterrorism and Pandemic Insurance

Project BioShield is a national form of bioterrorism and pandemic insurance. Funds and resources are set aside to plan and prepare for a biological attack or outbreak. Remember the Swine Flu of 2009? During the Swine Flu outbreak, when global media was clamoring that the Swine Flu might grow into a pandemic, the U.S. found itself without enough access to the medical resources and production capabilities to produce viable vaccines.

Health care triage ensued to ration available flu vaccines, and they were provided only to those in the most risky demographics (expectant mothers, youth under 24 years of age, and the elderly). Many citizens found themselves unable to receive a Swine Flu vaccine, increasing their vulnerability to the disease and creating the potential for a much larger pandemic to evolve. Fortunately, the Swine Flu epidemic turned out to be much less severe than feared; but it could have been far worse. Some estimates put the potential body count of a bioterror attack as high as 400,000, with the potential to do $2 trillion in economic damage.

Most importantly, the funding cuts to Project Bioshield emerged with a paucity of public discussion. It's one thing if a national discussion came to the conclusion that foregoing bioterrorism insurance was not in America's financial or health interest; it's quite another when important national security legislation is relegated to the back page. The affordability of national security is imperative, as is the affordability of other domestic social prospects. Therefore, public discussion of these important issues should be paramount. Otherwise, the transparency and accountability of taxpayers' dollars, and their personal health and safety, is diminished.

In the event of an attack, it would take two or three days for a bioterrorism attack to be confirmed. There would be a need for rapid transportation and distribution of the vaccine to inoculation dispensing locations. Time is of the essence. If countermeasures are not immediately available for distribution, the outbreak spreads and more people become infected. Cutting funding from Project BioShield limits America's ability to rapidly respond to bioterror events and pandemic outbreaks. That is a very big risk to take, and one with which many citizens may not be comfortable. The burden of proof is on Congress to demonstrate that bioterror and pandemic outbreaks are not a major risk to the nation's health and economy before cutting countermeasure insurance. Unfortunately, this contradicts many recent Congressional reports that claim the risks are clear and present.

Not Theoretical, but Highly Practical

The need to preserve our biological defenses is not theoretical, but highly practical. Consider the following scenario. The news media features the high likelihood that a bioterrorism attack has occurred. The government counter-bioterrorism strategy is to have the public wait for public health instruction. The White House Bioterrorism Roles and Responsibilities document, in the section on the Responsibilities of Individuals and Families, advises the public to: be prepared to follow public health guidance. This is good general advice, but it may break down, if and when an actual catastrophic bioterrorism event occurs.

In this scenario, the agitated public has two options: wait for government guidance; or self-help, if possible. The more likely option would be the latter—to get a countermeasure drug from a drugstore or other source, either with or without a doctor's prescription. Prudent preparation suggests that individuals and families stockpile a supply of antibiotics in their home before there is a bioterrorism attack. However, this would be a criminal act because either advocating stockpiling or unlawful use of prescription drugs is prohibited under current federal food and drug laws. The government's rationale is that "hoarding" countermeasure drugs and unprescribed drug use contributes to antibiotic resistance; but, the government bases this rationale on the assumption that adequate countermeasures will be available in the emergency stockpile, and that the government can quickly and efficiently distribute the countermeasures to the effected population. Prudent preparation and self-help in the first 72 hours of a biological emergency is common sense, and the public is justifiably dubious about the government's ability to perform in the event of a crisis, particularly if the emergency stockpile from BioShield is diminished.

The incursion into the BioShield stockpile is clearly cause for concern. The irony in all of this is that Congress and the [Barack] Obama administration recently passed the sweeping Health Care Reform Bill, which requires that all citizens must have health insurance. Without insurance, the costs of a medical problem could skyrocket, leaving the patient physically and financially devastated. Unfortunately, the same standard is not being applied to national bioterrorism insurance. Why is the insurance standard higher for the American citizen than it is for the national government? The House proposal suggests the United States can risk not paying its bioterrorism insurance premium.

| "To this day, the [stockpile] has no doses of a next-generation anthrax vaccine, nor any vaccines or drugs to defend against Ebola or plague."

Project BioShield Does Not Keep Americans Any Safer

Jon Cohen

In the following viewpoint, Jon Cohen asserts that Project BioShield, which earmarked about $5 billion toward biodefense research and development, has not made the nation significantly more secure. A new anthrax vaccine or countermeasures against other pathogens have yet to be delivered to stockpiles, he says. Furthermore, Cohen maintains that investments in pharmaceutical companies have failed to produce preventatives and treatments. For Project BioShield to be successful, he concludes, it must balance terrorist and natural threats and improve the cooperation of federal health and defense agencies. The author is a correspondent for Science *magazine and has contributed to the* New York Times Magazine, Atlantic Monthly, *and other publications.*

As you read, consider the following questions:

    1. According to Cohen, how many health care workers

Jon Cohen, "Reinventing Project Bioshield," *Science*, vol. 333, no. 6047, September 2, 2011, pp. 1216–1218. Copyright © 2011 by the American Association of the Advancement of Science. All rights reserved. Reproduced by permission.

volunteered for the smallpox vaccination program in 2003?

2. Aside from stockpiles of anthrax and smallpox vaccines, what type of acquisitions have been made under Project BioShield, as described by Cohen?

3. Why did the Department of Defense and Health of Human Services not continue working together in the program, as explained in the viewpoint?

In fall 2001, a few weeks after terrorists shook the world by flying commercial airliners into the Twin Towers, a second wave of attacks hit the United States. They caused far less harm but triggered powerful aftershocks of fear. Envelopes containing anthrax spores, sent to several news outlets and two U.S. senators, infected twenty-two people and killed five of them. Protecting against future bioterrorism attacks became a top priority for the government, and in his 2003 State of the Union address President George W. Bush announced the creation of Project BioShield. This "major research and production effort to guard our people against bioterrorism," Bush said, would "quickly make available effective vaccines and treatments against agents like anthrax, botulinum toxin, Ebola, and plague."

Congress passed legislation to establish Project BioShield the next year, creating a special $5.6 billion fund for the Department of Health and Human Services (HHS) to entice the most qualified pharmaceutical and biotechnology companies to invest in products that otherwise had no commercial market. The flagship product, specifically singled out by Bush when he signed the bill into law at a White House ceremony, would be an improved version of the anthrax vaccine long used by the Department of Defense (DOD) to protect troops. Bush said HHS "has already taken steps to purchase 75 million doses" of this new vaccine, which the U.S. Army Medical Research Institute of Infectious Diseases had been developing for over a decade. The new version would have fewer side effects and be easier to administer. The White House said it expected the vaccine to become part of the Strategic National Stockpile (SNS)—a repository of medicines run by HHS's Centers for Disease Control and Prevention for use in a public health emergency—the next year.

Little Traction

To this day, the SNS has no doses of a next-generation anthrax vaccine, nor any vaccines or drugs to defend against Ebola or plague. No major pharmaceutical companies have supplied Project BioShield, and the small biotech companies involved often have had difficulty with large-scale manufacturing and regulatory issues. Congress has also transferred $1.4 billion of BioShield money—more than 25%—to other projects. "What you're left with is a great idea that was terribly flawed and unfortunately didn't get the big splash it wanted," says Robert Kadlec, a career U.S. Air Force officer who worked on biodefense for the George W. Bush White House and now is a director with the management consulting firm PRTM in Washington, D.C. "If this were a business and we ran it like in the private sector, we'd have been out of business a long time ago."

Project BioShield has delivered on some of its promises, making one-time purchases of drugs and vaccines that were already far along the development pipeline, and Kadlec and others emphasize that it has steadily improved over its seven years of existence. It is also just one part of a massive post-9/11 scientific push to find and develop new medical countermeasures against chemical, biological, radiological, and nuclear threats. But taking stock of Project BioShield, many see an underlying tension that has bedeviled it from inception: HHS and DOD—the other main government agency that funds R&D to prepare the country for bioterrorist attack—have distinct needs, mindsets, and agendas. And HHS, the new rich kid on the block in the wake of 9/11, has had some difficulty tapping DOD expertise and simultaneously charting its own course. "DOD and HHS have very different requirements," says Michael Kurilla, who heads the Office of Biodefense Research Affairs at the U.S. National Institute of Allergy and Infectious Diseases (NIAID) in Bethesda, Maryland.

Kurilla says the architects of Project BioShield, which was spearheaded by then-Vice President Dick Cheney, tried to adapt the DOD approach to protecting troops to the broader population: Vaccinate them against anthrax, smallpox, botulism, tularemia, and plague. "There was an expectation to vaccinate everyone in the country and take the biothreat off the table," he says. But this ambitious goal gained little traction, both because the small companies that came forward stumbled in producing preventives and treatments, and because HHS concluded that a program for the public had to take a different tack from the one for troops. "The initial focus and orientation for the program has changed dramatically," Kurilla says.

BioShield, Take One

In a foretaste of the problems confronting Project BioShield, the national smallpox vaccination program for health care workers tanked in 2003, the year BioShield was launched. The goal was to protect some 500,000 of these "first responders," but the program attracted only 40,000 volunteers. For civilians, "taking the threat off the table" held little attraction when people weighed the risk of vaccine side effects against the perceived risk of a smallpox attack. The writing was on the wall: If the nascent BioShield emphasized prevention, it would face similar challenges.

When Congress held a hearing that March about the proposed Project BioShield, experts flagged what they saw as another unrealistic aspect of the master plan. James Baker, an immunologist at the University of Michigan, Ann Arbor, who previously worked in the U.S. Army on its anthrax vaccine program, warned that the proposed project would likely attract only small companies with little experience, as the government had made no long-term commitment to continue purchasing any of the countermeasures after the initial investment. "No large pharmaceutical company is going to come in unless there's a defined market and a defined revenue stream that accompanies the contract," Baker says. . . . He's disappointed but not the least surprised by what Project BioShield has accomplished. "We haven't moved as far as we thought we would have, given the time and money involved."

Part of the problem, Kadlec says, is that from the outset BioShield didn't have sufficient funding. "Investing $5.6 billion for pharmaceutical and biomedical manufacturing is spit in the bucket," he says, noting that it can cost up to $1 billion to develop a drug or vaccine.

Project BioShield's first investment brought the dilemma painfully to the fore. HHS awarded $879 million—a huge chunk of its budget—to a fledgling biotechnology company, VaxGen, to make 75 million doses of a new anthrax vaccine. The decades-old anthrax vaccine, made from growing *Bacillus anthracis* and then isolating what's called protective antigen, must be administered in a half-dozen doses followed by annual boosters and causes many side effects. Since the 1980s, DOD had been working on a purer vaccine that contains a genetically engineered, recombinant version of protective antigen. But for a variety of technical, manufacturing, and funding reasons, the DOD project had stalled, and VaxGen—a company best known for an AIDS vaccine that had failed in human trials—acquired the technology and began developing its own version that promised to be safer and provide protection with three doses at most.

Nearly Destroying the Program

In December 2006, HHS canceled the VaxGen contract because the company had difficulty making a stable vaccine that met U.S. Food and Drug Administration (FDA) requirements for a planned clinical trial. "They had lots of inexperience in major things, including business, the ability to scale up a product, and the skills to deal with the regulatory pathway, which was nebulous in many areas," says Robin Robinson, who at the time

Project BioShield Acquisitions

BioShield added several vaccines and drugs to the Strategic National Stockpile, but critics expected more.

Product	Company	Contracted Doses	Funding
Anthrax Monoclonal Antibody*	Human Genome Sciences	65,000	$334 million
Anthrax Immune Globulin*	Cangene	10,000	$144 million
Anthrax Vaccine	Emergent	28.75 million	$691 million
Recombinant Protective Antigen Anthrax Vaccine	VaxGen	75 million, terminated	$2 million
Botulism Antitoxin*	Cangene	117,000	$476 million
Smallpox Vaccine (MVA)*	Bavarian Nordic	20 million	$505 million
Smallpox Antiviral*	SIGA Technologies	1.7 million	$433 million
Potassium Iodide (pediatric radio-nuclear exposure)	Fleming	4.8 million	$18 million
IV Calcium/ Zinc DTPA (radio-nuclear exposure)	Akorn	473,710	$22 million
TOTAL			**$2.625 billion**

*Lacks FDA approval

TAKEN FROM: Jon Cohen, "Reinventing Project BioShield," *Science*, vol. 333, no. 6047, Sept. 2, 2011.

had recently taken over HHS's influenza and emerging disease program after a twelve-year stint in the vaccine industry. "It nearly destroyed the program." (VaxGen appealed the contract cancellation and later settled with HHS out of court.)

Congress, well aware of Project BioShield's shaky start, passed legislation that same month that revamped the effort. A special HHS division, the Biomedical Advanced Research and Development Authority (BARDA), would now run the project. Modeled on a similar DOD division, "BARDA will bring innovation to a process that is simply too slow to combat terrorist activities or Mother Nature," said the bill's key Senate sponsor, Richard Burr (R–NC). In addition to coordinating efforts to combat both bioterror and emerging infectious diseases, BARDA would fund earlier stage products and offer companies milestone payments to help them make it through the middle stage of R&D, the "valley of death" when many promising projects run out of funding. BARDA could also help companies scale up for commercial manufacturing and complete the testing needed for FDA approval.

Bush signed the bill into law on 19 December 2006, the same day HHS canceled the VaxGen contract. Robinson's branch moved under BARDA, and in April 2008, he became its first director.

BioShield, Take Two

Project BioShield's contributions to the SNS to date are modest; they include mostly products contracted before BARDA came into existence. The largest purchases have been 28.75 million doses of the old-fashioned anthrax vaccine and 20 million doses of a new smallpox vaccine that's safe for people who have compromised immune systems. Beyond that, every acquisition is for a postexposure treatment instead of a preventative, and the number of doses—which is set by the Department of Homeland Security through a process known as material threat assessment—can protect against only limited attacks. There are fewer than 6 million doses of a treatment for exposure to radiation, and only enough botulinum antitoxin to treat about 100,000 people. Novel anthrax treatments, which theoretically would supplement existing antibiotics, total 75,000. A smallpox antiviral would treat 1.7 million. Several of these products have yet to receive FDA approval, and all have expiration dates; as a result, the U.S. government is the only market and will have to pay top dollar to keep fresh supplies in stock.

Two reports last year evaluated the U.S. government's overall efforts to protect against a bioattack, and their conclusions were bleak. Although the reports focus on far more than BioShield, the project did not fare well. The congressionally mandated, bipartisan Commission on the Prevention of Weapons of Mass Destruction Proliferation and Terrorism issued a report card in January 2010 that gave the government an "F" for its efforts to "enhance the nation's capabilities for rapid response to prevent biological attacks from inflicting mass casualties." It warned that both the White House and Congress had repeatedly tried to "raid" Project BioShield funds "for programs not associated with National Security." (Congress transferred $137 million to combat pandemic flu and another $304 million to NIAID in part to support basic research for emerging infectious diseases.)

The second report came from the National Biodefense Science Board, which guides HHS on scientific and technical matters related to chemical, biological, radiological, and nuclear weapons. The board's March 2010 report, *Where Are the Countermeasures?*, called the entire federal program "a good effort conducted by talented people." But it criticized HHS for having "not fully tapped the talent" of DOD and said the program lacks strong centralized leadership and coordination. It further complained that there's no unified national strategy to focus on top threats and best responses. "America expects orchestration within HHS's scientific endeavors, not cacophony," the report jabbed. "If achieving national [medical countermeasure] goals is likened to climbing a mountain, then most of the mountain remains to be climbed."

Robinson contends that many people have held Project BioShield to unfair standards, noting that it developed nine products in seven years. "A company would be unbelievably successful if it were able to do this," he says. What's more, he says, companies regularly have hiccups or failures, but in Project BioShield, "we're expected to have none."

Robinson says the country is safer now. "We have things that were not available in the United States seven or eight years ago. That's a pretty good measure of success. If we had any of those [bioterror] events, we would be using those products." And he says BARDA has developed a much more diversified portfolio that will fill the SNS with a wide array of new medicines. "We're on the right course," he assures.

As Project BioShield has evolved, it has developed a broader target that's more attractive to industry. "We're moving away from one-drug, one-bug solutions," NIAID's Kurilla says. Robinson notes that BARDA awarded several contracts for drugs to combat strains of anthrax, tularemia, and plague that have developed resistance to existing antibiotics. These same antibiotics have applications beyond biodefense: They can be used to treat people who have acquired multidrug-resistant infections. "Large pharma basically had shut their projects on these antibiotics because they didn't see the markets," Robinson says. Now that Project BioShield has offered what looks like a more sustainable market, he says, big pharma "has picked up on that." In the past two years, BARDA has also funded new efforts to make a recombinant anthrax vaccine and novel treatments for skin and lung problems caused by chemical or radiation attacks.

BioShield, Take Three

The centerpiece of the next incarnation of BARDA and Project BioShield is the result of yet another review by HHS of its medical countermeasures for bioterrorism and emerging infections—

and again highlights tensions with DOD. The review, conducted by all involved HHS divisions, concluded that HHS should establish Centers of Innovation for Advanced Development and Manufacturing, which would essentially be manufacturing plants to help small companies produce commercial quantities of drugs and vaccines.

HHS initially hoped BARDA would work with DOD to build these plants, but the two agencies now plan to contract out their own facilities. "DOD and HHS started together but decided for reasons beyond me to go separately," Kadlec says. "I have no confidence that we're looking for benefits and cost savings and leveraging expertise and scarce resources." Robinson said DOD's unique mission to protect soldiers with vaccines against potential bioweapons ultimately led the department to go its own way; none of what it manufactures will go into the SNS.

So far, only HHS has issued a solicitation to build the new centers, which could manufacture anything from chemical, biological, radiological, and nuclear countermeasures to pandemic flu vaccines. Robinson says he expects HHS to issue contracts early next year and that construction should take eighteen months to three years. "You can't do it any faster," he says. "Concrete doesn't set very well when you start putting stuff on top of it too soon."

Ultimately, Project BioShield's fate depends on funding. The initial legislation expires in 2013, and a bill now in the House of Representatives would keep the effort alive until 2019, adding $2.8 billion to its coffers. "It's going to be more successful as we go forward because we've made the course corrections midstream to put the dollars where they are needed," Robinson says.

Project BioShield's future success will also likely depend on its ability to balance natural versus intentional threats and better define how it can work with DOD to protect the country if the unthinkable happens. "The real problem," the University of Michigan's Baker says, "is that none of these agencies seem to play well with each other."

> *"The vaccine will greatly increase the chances of soldiers surviving exposure to inhalational anthrax."*

The Anthrax Vaccine Is Safe and Protects Military Personnel

Military Vaccine (MILVAX) Agency

In the following viewpoint, The Military Vaccine (MILVAX) Agency claims that the anthrax vaccine safely and effectively protects military personnel against the pathogen. The agency contends that anthrax remains the most important bioweapon due to its lethality and ease of production—an attack can be unpredictable and released through unconventional means—requiring vaccinations for US forces at risk. Scientific evidence demonstrates that the vaccine prevents anthrax regardless of the path of exposure, MILVAX suggests, and should protect against different bioengineered strains. MILVAX supports immunization programs for service members and provides educational resources for healthcare practitioners in defense.

As you read, consider the following questions:

1. How many Department of Defense (DoD) personnel have been vaccinated against anthrax since March 1998?

Military Vaccine (MILVAX) Agency, Office of the Army Surgeon General, US Army, "Anthrax Vaccine Immunization Program (AVIP) Questions and Answers," August 27, 2009. www.anthrax.ods.mil.

2. As told by MILVAX, which service members are most at risk of exposure to anthrax?

3. What evidence does the agency cite for the effectiveness of the vaccine against the inhalation of anthrax?

W *hy is anthrax vaccination needed?*

Anthrax is highly lethal and relatively easy to produce in large quantities for use as a weapon. Anthrax spores are easily spread in the air over a large area, and can be stored and remain viable for a long time. For this reason, anthrax may be the most important biological warfare threat facing U.S. forces. The intelligence community believes several countries currently have or are developing an offensive biological warfare capability using anthrax. However, given the ease with which anthrax can be produced, the threat could come from anywhere. For that reason, U.S. Forces may have little or no warning before an anthrax attack, which could be delivered by unconventional means. As a result, U.S. military forces around the world face a very real threat of a surprise anthrax attack. On February 24, 2004, CIA [Central Intelligence Agency] Director George Tenet told the Senate Select Intelligence Committee: "Although gaps in our understanding remain, we see al-Qaeda's program to produce anthrax as one of the most immediate terrorist CBRN [chemical, biological, radiological, nuclear] threats we are likely to face."

Has any country ever used anthrax as a weapon?

There is some evidence that the Japanese used anthrax as a biological weapon (BW) in China during World War II.

Since then, several countries are believed to have incorporated anthrax spores into biological weapons. Intelligence analysts believe that at least seven potential adversaries have an offensive BW capability to deliver anthrax—twice the number of countries when the 1972 Biological and Toxin Weapons Convention (BTWC) took effect. The BTWC was designed to prohibit such activity.

Iraq admitted to the United Nations in 1995 that it loaded anthrax spores into warheads during the Gulf War. In the post-cold war era, the former Soviet Union admitted to having enough anthrax on hand to kill every person on the planet several times over. The accidental aerosolized release of anthrax spores from a military microbiology facility in the former Soviet Union city of Sverdlovsk in 1979 resulted in at least seventy-nine cases of anthrax infection and sixty-eight human deaths and demonstrated the lethal potential of anthrax aerosols. Members of Aum Shinrikyo, the group responsible for the 1995 Tokyo sarin attack, reportedly experimented with biological agents in Japan before resorting to chemical agents. A lengthy article in the May 26, 1998, edition of the *New York Times* reported that members of Aum Shinrikyo released anthrax spores and botulinum toxin in Tokyo, Yokohama, and Yokosuka in 1990, targeting Japanese government and U.S. Navy facilities. Fortunately, no one was injured in these events.

Anthrax spores have also been used as a weapon inside the United States by unknown terrorists in the Fall of 2001. The attack killed five people and infected at least seventeen others.

Has anthrax vaccine ever been used in the past? How often?

Yes, since licensure in November 1970, anthrax vaccine has been administered to people at risk (both civilian and military)—veterinarians, laboratory workers, and some people working with livestock for several decades. The manufacturer and FDA [Food and Drug Administration] report that about 68,000 doses of anthrax vaccine were distributed between 1974 and 1989. The Army has purchased anthrax vaccine since its approval by the FDA in 1970, for use by about 1,500 at-risk laboratory workers. Anthrax vaccine was administered during the Gulf War to about 150,000 Service members, to protect U.S. forces against the threat of Iraq's biological weapons. The DoD [Department of Defense] vaccinated over 1.5 million DoD personnel with over 5.9 million doses since the beginning of the AVIP [Anthrax Vaccine Immunization Program] in March 1998.

Anthrax in Warfare

How are biological agents deployed?

Biological agents can be dispersed in many ways, ranging from mailed envelopes, intentional human vectors, spray devices, bombs, to ballistic missiles. Biological agents are often hard to detect. Symptoms are delayed. Without preventive medical efforts such as vaccination, the results can be devastating and widespread. A 1993 report by the U.S. Congressional Office of Technology Assessment estimated that between 130,000 and 3 million deaths could follow the aerosolized release of 100 kg of anthrax spores upwind of the Washington, DC area—truly a weapon of mass destruction. An anthrax aerosol would be odorless, invisible, and capable of traveling many miles.

Has the threat of biological warfare changed?

The threat of biological warfare has been a risk to U.S. forces for many years. The threat of anthrax weapons in the hands of adversarial countries remains. But anthrax was used as a biological weapon in the United States in fall 2001 by unknown terrorists. Delivering anthrax was as simple as putting it in an envelope and dropping it in a mailbox. DoD analysts maintain an updated evaluation of the level of threat, adjusting the information as necessary to reflect the risk to U.S. operations. Assessment of the potential offensive biological threat facing American Service members indicates it is necessary to have a robust biological defense program today. The threat is real and the consequences are grave. On 16 October, 2006, Assistant Secretary of Defense for

Health Affairs William Winkenwerder said, "... anthrax remains a deadly infection that's been used as a bioterrorism weapon against our own population. The threat environment and unpredictable nature of terrorism makes it necessary to include biological warfare defense as part of our force protection measures."

Who is at greater risk from a biological attack? Soldiers? Sailors? Airmen? Marines? Front line? Rear area? Logistical units?

Anthrax weapons have the potential to contaminate wide areas of the battlefield. It is difficult to determine who would be at a greater risk from a biological threat. All Service members meeting the criteria to receive the vaccine need to be protected, regardless of Service, specialty, or location within higher threat areas.

What preparations have been made to respond to an anthrax release in a high-threat area?

We are taking necessary steps to develop optimal protection against the threat of anthrax and other potential bio-weapon agents, including improved intelligence, detection, surveillance capabilities, protective clothing and equipment, new generation vaccines, and other medical countermeasures. In addition, we have stockpiled antibiotics in pre-positioned locations and medical personnel are better educated in the treatment of anthrax.

If we vaccinate against anthrax, couldn't our adversaries just switch to a different biological weapon?

If the DoD anthrax vaccination program causes adversaries to switch to a different weapon, it can be considered a success. Other biological weapons are less stable, less predictable, or less effective than anthrax weapons.

Are vaccines being developed for other biological agents?

Yes. As potential biological warfare threats are identified, DoD works with other government agencies and industry partners to develop medical countermeasures. Vaccines are being developed, whenever appropriate, for all validated biological threat agents. . . .

Scientific Evidence of Vaccine Effectiveness

Why do we think the anthrax vaccine will protect people if anthrax inhalation occurs? What scientific evidence do we have?

This vaccine prevents anthrax regardless of route of exposure. Based on human and animal data, the National Academy of Sciences' Institute of Medicine concluded in March 2002 that anthrax vaccine is "an effective vaccine for the protection of humans against anthrax, including inhalational anthrax, caused by all known or plausible engineered strains of *Bacillus anthracis.*" The original Brachman and CDC [Centers for Disease Control and Prevention] studies of anthrax vaccine in textile workers proved that the vaccine protected against anthrax. The calculations performed in that study combined the cutaneous (skin) and inhalational forms of anthrax infection that occurred. No inhalational anthrax occurred among the vaccinated workers, while five cases of inhalational anthrax occurred among workers who had not been vaccinated. The total number of inhalation cases was judged too few to show statistically conclusive proof of protection by itself. However, results from several animal studies provide additional evidence that the vaccine protects against anthrax challenge with hundreds of times the lethal dose of anthrax by inhalation. This information coupled with the encouraging results of the effectiveness and immune response in humans assures us that the vaccine will greatly increase the chances of soldiers surviving exposure to inhalational anthrax. When full immunization is combined with proper use of protective masks, detection devices, surveillance and post-exposure treatment with antibiotics, the threat is even further reduced.

I heard that the vaccine used in the 1962 Brachman study isn't the same as the vaccine used today. Is that true?

Yes, it is true that the current vaccine has more protective antigen (PA) in it than Brachman's vaccine formula, and also that the current vaccine is more highly purified than the vaccine used in the Brachman study. Between the time of the Brachman study and the licensing of the vaccine produced in Lansing, the conditions under which the anthrax bacteria were cultured were changed. These changes resulted in a purer, more potent vaccine. Government authorities were aware of and approved the changes at the time the license application was considered in 1970. The independent, civilian review panel advising the FDA was aware of the changes, and described them in its 1985 report. Both vaccine formulas are based on protective antigen (PA), the key protein common to all strains of anthrax.

Levels of Protection

What will happen if personnel are exposed to anthrax before they gain immunity through vaccination?

Personnel will be treated with antibiotics if there is a known exposure to anthrax before gaining immunity through vaccination. Antibiotics are effective in treating animals, including primates, exposed to inhalational anthrax, but only if started before symptoms develop. This would usually mean starting antibiotics in the first twenty-four hours after exposure. Unfortunately, service members may not know they have been exposed until symptoms develop; by then, the infection is nearly always fatal within a few days, whether antibiotics are given or not. The best protection to counter inhalational anthrax is the use of the anthrax vaccine

A Safer, Cell-Free Vaccine

A 1904 study demonstrating that extracts from edema fluid from anthrax lesions provided protection in animals led to the eventual development of a safer, cell-free vaccine for humans. The Anthrax vaccine now used in the United States, BioThrax.

Alan L. Menick, Biological, Chemical, and Radiological Terrorism: Emergency Preparedness and Response for the Primary Care Physician. *New York: Springer Science and Business Media, 2008.*

combined with the appropriate Mission Oriented Protective Posture (MOPP), including protective clothing and detection equipment.

If you receive all the shots, are you 100% protected?

No medication, no vaccine is 100% effective. The antibodies that result from any vaccine theoretically could be overwhelmed if one is exposed to extremely large doses of any pathogen. Even if vaccinated, one may not be completely safe if one is close to the point of release of the biologic agent. Antibiotics for such people will offer additional protection. That's why vaccination is only one part of force health protection efforts, which also includes protective gear and detection equipment. For continued protection, annual booster doses are required.

Does anthrax vaccine protect against disease if someone inhales anthrax spores?

The original studies of anthrax vaccine showed 93% fewer anthrax infections (combining both cutaneous and inhalational cases of anthrax) among vaccinated people, compared to unvaccinated people. In those original studies, no cases of inhaled (inhalation) anthrax occurred among vaccine recipients, while five cases of anthrax occurred among unvaccinated or incompletely vaccinated people. This difference involved too few people to be statistically conclusive, although the trend is obvious. It is unethical to intentionally expose human beings to inhaled anthrax to test the vaccine. Instead, anthrax vaccine was tested on rhesus monkeys. After sixty-five animals received one or two doses of vaccine, 95% survived aerosol challenge in full health. One animal died from anthrax exposure two years after the second dose of vaccine. This illustrates the importance of annual booster doses of anthrax vaccine. These data lead us to expect that anthrax vaccine would be quite effective in preventing inhaled anthrax.

How long does it take after the first shot before protection begins?

Antibodies begin to develop within a week or two after the first dose of vaccine. Protection levels increase as shots in the series are given, like walking up a set of stairs. The entire six-shot series is needed for full protection as licensed by the Food & Drug Administration.

Will this anthrax vaccine protect soldiers from all forms of anthrax, including the ones reportedly developed in Russia?

Every disease-causing strain of *Bacillus anthracis* causes anthrax disease via the same protein. The vaccine produces antibodies that neutralize that protein. The National Academy of Sciences' Institute of Medicine concluded in March 2002 that "it is unlikely that either naturally occurring or anthrax strains with bioengineered protective antigen could both evade AVA [the US anthrax vaccine] and cause the toxicity associated with anthrax." DoD is aware of the Russian research effort recently reported in a British scientific journal. Russian scientists reported using technology to introduce two foreign genes into anthrax. The potential for a genetically altered virulent organism is of concern to us and we are anxious to learn more about this organism. Hamsters vaccinated with the Russian live attenuated anthrax vaccine were not resistant to challenge with their engineered strain. There are substantive scientific questions about this report. First, the validity of the animal model that the Russians used needs to be addressed, because hamsters may not be predictive of results in other animals (including humans). Second, the strain produced may not be stable, a fact the Russians admit. An unstable organism would not be a candidate for weaponization. There have been ongoing efforts by OSD [Office of the Secretary of Defense] Cooperative Threat Reduction Program, the National Academy of Sciences, and the International Science and Technology Center to evaluate the possibility of a potential threat from genetically modified strains, and to ensure that our vaccine is effective against them. We believe that the current anthrax vaccine would be effective against altered genetic strains based on the biologic principles of the U.S. vaccine, which is different from the Russian vaccine.

Is the anthrax vaccine licensed for use against biological agents?

The anthrax vaccine is licensed for people at risk for exposure to anthrax spores. Biological weapons are designed to deliver aerosolized anthrax spores that will result in inhalational anthrax. The FDA concurs that the use of the anthrax vaccine to protect against inhalational anthrax is consistent with indications for use of the vaccine.

What is the FDA's position about the effectiveness of anthrax vaccine?

For years, the FDA has held that anthrax vaccine prevents anthrax infection regardless of the route of exposure. On December 15, 2005, the Food and Drug Administration released a Final Rule and Final Order for anthrax vaccine. After reviewing extensive scientific evidence and carefully considering comments from the public, the FDA determined that anthrax vaccine is safe and effective in preventing anthrax disease regardless of route of exposure, including inhalation anthrax.

"Questions on general efficacy and animal immunization aside, how well does the human vaccine protect against the 33 known natural strains of anthrax?"

The Use of the Anthrax Vaccine on Military Personnel Is Problematic

Wade-Hahn Chan

In the following article, the author contends that although the anthrax vaccine is mandatory for military personnel, it is unknown how effective the vaccine is against the thirty-three different strains of anthrax. There may still be unknown risks associated with the vaccine, he reports. Wade-Hahn Chan is a writer for Insight on the News.

As you read, consider the following questions:
1. According to the article, what is squalene?
2. According to the viewpoint, is there a chance the anthrax vaccine would not protect against inhalation anthrax?

3. What is the name of the primary human study of the anthrax vaccine?

The Department of Defense (DoD) has revived its Anthrax Vaccine Immunization Program (AVIP). Emboldened by a report issued last March by the Institute of Medicine (IOM), DoD made the anthrax vaccine part of the mandated protection for military personnel and emergency workers. DoD health-affairs spokesman Jim Turner says the program will make the vaccine "a condition of employment" for those at high risk of anthrax exposure.

But can this vaccine be trusted to be both safe and effective? Certainly there have been questions about its long-term systemic effects and even whether it causes birth defects. As *Insight* was the first to report, it contains a suspect amount of the ingredient squalene, an oily substance otherwise used for silicone breast implants, that may cause adverse side effects . . . .

An article published in the August issue of Experimental & Molecular Pathology by medical researchers Pamela Asa, Russell Wilson and Robert Garry shows that in some cases there have been adverse reactions to the vaccine similar to known squalene side effects found by other researchers. These include joint and muscle pain, dizziness, chronic headaches, low-grade fevers, chronic fatigue, weakness, seizures, memory loss and cognitive problems. However, the health-affairs wing of DoD as well as the Food and Drug Administration (FDA) both have dismissed such concerns and stated that studies already are in progress to evaluate the safety of the vaccine administered to troops.

Besides, say advocates of the vaccine, isn't it better to provide some protection from weaponized anthrax for U.S. servicemen and first-responders than to have none?

Critics' View of the Anthrax Vaccine

Not if the anthrax vaccine doesn't give much protection in the first place, say critics. And the anthrax vaccine may not protect against inhalation anthrax. A spokesman for FDRs Center for Biologics Regulation (CBER) says the label of the anthrax vaccine "does not contradict" protection against infection by inhalation anthrax, but the vaccine only is licensed by FDA to protect against infection by cutaneous (skin) anthrax.

That's true for men at least—no one knows for certain how it will affect women. While the product label advises against giving the vaccine to pregnant women, no epidemiological tests have been done to evaluate how the vaccine reacts in a female body, pregnant or not, or even what it will do in the case of future pregnancies. The label says it's not known whether the vaccine "can cause fetal harm when administered to a pregnant woman or can affect reproduction capacity." Is this serious? Past safety monitoring shows that local and systemic reactions occur 50 percent more often in females than in males.

The primary human study of the vaccine is known as the Brachman test, run between 1955 and 1959 on wool-sorting workers in New England. DoD says that, based the Brachman findings, the vaccine is "92.5 percent effective" against cutaneous anthrax in the wool-mill setting. This suggests that of 100 people vaccinated for exposure to anthrax spores, seven to eight would contract cutaneous anthrax. The tests helped pave the way for an FDA license for the vaccine in 1970—a license for cutaneous-anthrax infections only.

Vaccine Effectiveness

There was an outbreak of inhalation anthrax also, but with too few cases to reach any conclusion about the effectiveness of the vaccine against anthrax contracted in that form. There also were too few female workers in the Brachman study to allow for conclusions, and what data there were about the women weren't separated from those on the men.

The only other data to establish the effectiveness of the vaccine against inhalation anthrax are animal tests. The DoD claims that five studies on rhesus monkeys were done in the mid-nineties. The monkeys were given one or two shots of the vaccine, resulting in 62 of 65 surviving otherwise lethal doses of inhalation anthrax, whereas all 18 of the unvaccinated monkeys died. In rabbit tests, 114 of 117 vaccinated rabbits survived inhalation anthrax, whereas all 28 unvaccinated rabbits died.

However, questions arose even from those conducting the studies. In one of the 1996 rhesus monkey tests, for instance, it was concluded that the findings might mean "immune mechanisms against inhalation anthrax may vary in different animal species."

Questions on general efficacy and animal immunization aside, how well does the human vaccine protect against the 33 known natural strains of anthrax? Turner says the vaccine "protects against all known strains of anthrax" but it is clear from other data that this simply isn't true. In 1988, Dr. Bruce Ivins, part of the U.S. Army Medical Research Institute of Infectious Diseases (USAMRIID) bacteriology division, wrote in the Clinical Immunology Newsletter that there is "some evidence indicating that [the vaccine] may have diminished efficacy against certain virulent strains of [anthrax]." . . .

Lack of Testing

Nor have there been any tests on mixed strains—that is, cocktails of multiple strains. Two Russian anthrax scientists published a 1997 article in Vaccine detailing their work in creating a genetically modified anthrax strain. Their Obolensk lab managed to produce a strain without the gene that produces protective antigen (PA), the protein that causes the body to produce antibodies. The lack of PA made the genetically altered anthrax strain immune to antibiotics when tested on hamsters, which also suggests the current DoD vaccine may not be able to protect against it. The AVIP advocates using both the vaccine and antibiotics for an added layer of protection. . . .

Is it worth having both a pre-exposure program such as the anthrax vaccine combined with a postexposure treatment such as a super-antibiotic? Not exactly. In the mid-nineties a study done at Fort Detrick, Md., compared anthrax-infected rabbits that were treated with an antibiotic alone with a group treated with both the anthrax vaccine and antibiotics together. It was concluded that one treatment worked about as well as the other.

Then don't these tests show that the vaccine provides at least some protection? Only if the vaccine in the Brachman tests is the same one U.S. personnel currently are receiving. While the FDA says the current vaccine is "similar" to the vaccine used in the Brachman tests, both the strain used to grow the vaccine as well as its formulation are different. . . .

Outdated Technology and Contaminants

In a 1999 report rifled Chemical and Biological Terrorism, IOM says, "the current vaccine, made by outdated technology . . . is an impure mixture of bacterial products. Antigen content is variable from lot to lot due to the manufacturing process and the instability to precisely quantify antigenic components" And, says IOM, "the requirement for multiple doses (six shots in 18 months and an annual booster shot) is a serous limitation, especially if the vaccine is needed for use in response to exposure of a civilian population." . . .

"There are no studies being done because FDA has already approved the vaccine's efficacy," says Turner. Those taking the vaccine will be tracked to ensure that they remain close to their immunization schedule, but Turner says to the best of his knowledge no long-term epidemiological studies are being conducted.

But some critics, including FDA officials contacted by Insight, worry that an FDA discovery in 1999 that found trace amounts of squalene in various batches of anthrax vaccine could cause illness because of the substance's known adjuvant properties.

"Something is wrong when we find a contaminant in the vaccine [lots tested] that shouldn't be there," an FDA official tells *Insight.* "That tells me an investigation should have been launched. It wasn't, because of pressure, and that's not right; this vaccine should not be used until DoD finds out how squalene got into those tested batches, whether other batches are contaminated and what are the health consequences from the contamination." . . .

Finally, if the United States is to pursue a counterterrorism public-health policy of pre-exposure vaccination rather than postexposure treatment, would this be extended to other bioterror agents as well? Say smallpox, polio or plague? Stay tuned.

> "We must fully embrace the spirit
> of 'all hazards' in [the Pandemic
> and All-Hazards Preparedness Act]
> by recognizing that almost every
> public health program contributes to
> preparedness."

Reauthorizing the Pandemic and All-Hazards Preparedness Act Will Help Protect Against Bioterrorism

Lowell P. Weicker

In 2006, the Pandemic and All-Hazards Preparedness Act *(PAHPA) was enacted, impacting the role and activities of the Department of Health and Human Services in national emergencies. In the following viewpoint, Lowell P. Weicker maintains that the reauthorization of PAHPA would address the critical gaps in the public health system to respond to a bioterrorist attack or dangerous outbreak. It would strengthen the public health preparedness workforce; modernize and unify biosurveillance and health information technology; improve the nation's approach to the research, development, and production of medical countermeasures; and*

Lowell P. Weicker, "Testimony of Governor Lowell P. Weicker, President of the Board of Directors, Trust for America's Health, Senate Committee on Health, Education, Labor and Pensions, A Nation Prepared: Strengthening Medical and Public Health Preparedness and Response," May 17, 2011. healthyamericans.org.

extend the surge capacity of hospitals and emergency management, he insists. Weicker is president of the board of directors of
Trust for America's Health, a nonpartisan, nonprofit advocacy for
disease prevention.

As you read, consider the following questions:
1. According to the author, by what percent has funding for
   public health preparedness declined over the last several
   years?
2. How does the author describe "situational awareness"?
3. What is the aim of the Hospital Preparedness Program
   (HPP)?

My name is Lowell P. Weicker, and I am President of the
Board of Directors of Trust for America's Health (TFAH),
a nonprofit, nonpartisan organization dedicated to saving lives
by protecting the health of every community and working to
make disease prevention a national priority. I am grateful for the
opportunity to submit testimony to the Committee on reauthorization of a groundbreaking piece of legislation, the Pandemic
and All-Hazards Preparedness Act (PAHPA).

PAHPA represented a major step in acknowledging and developing the role of America's public health system in preparing
for and responding to major emergencies, whether natural or
man-made. The reauthorization of PAHPA is an opportunity to
build more prepared and resilient communities, able to weather
a storm, contain its impact, and return to normal as quickly as
possible. I applaud the Committee for demonstrating its commitment to better preparing our nation for disasters.

I have two major points to make in my testimony today:

First, our nation faces continuing natural and man-made
threats that require an ongoing commitment to public health
preparedness. This is a national security threat—as direct as any
we face abroad. The death of Osama Bin-Laden does not erase

that threat; there are still very creative terrorists out there and our guard cannot be let down.

Second, we must fund public health preparedness with the same level of commitment as we have made to other national security priorities. This means: (a) we must assure reliable, predictable funding for public health preparedness, in contrast to the 27 percent decline faced over the last several years; (b) we must assure that state and local health departments are given flexibility to use all employees supported with federal funds during an emergency and not be hamstrung by categorical restrictions; (c) and we must fully embrace the spirit of "all hazards" in PAHPA by recognizing that almost every public health program contributes to preparedness. As our health care system modernizes— especially with regard to health information technology—we must be sure public health programs, such as biosurveillance, adapt as well, including by leveraging existing resources in more creative ways.

The public health system has always been integral in our response to natural disasters and terrorist attacks. Public health was on the frontlines of the response to 9-11 and to the anthrax attacks. It is as fundamental to the nation's security as our military and as fundamental to local protection as fire and rescue. Passage of PAHPA codified and expanded the federal government's support for this role. As a result of this legislation, and the investments that followed, our nation is more prepared than ever. We saw this in the response to the H1N1 outbreak in 2009, when nearly every state and jurisdiction implemented its pandemic influenza plan in response to the H1N1 outbreak, with activities including disease surveillance, ongoing communication updates, carrying out vaccination campaigns and the coordination of response efforts with partners.

Filling the Critical Gaps

In TFAH's 2010 report, *Ready or Not?*, we found that states had made enormous progress since the events of 2001 in planning for and responding to disasters. The Public Health Emergency Preparedness (PHEP) cooperative agreement and Hospital Preparedness Program (HPP), federal, state, and local attention to the role of public health in emergency preparedness, and real-world experiences such as the H1N1 outbreak have helped us bring preparedness to the next level. However, the report also found that the economic crisis is putting almost a decade of gains at serious risk. While emergency H1N1 and stimulus funds may have helped states weather the storm of the pandemic, we cannot continue to fund preparedness on a disaster-by-disaster basis. Our report found that 33 states and D.C. cut public health funding from fiscal years 2008–09 to 2009–10, with 18 of these states cutting funding for the second year in a row. In addition, federal support for public health preparedness was cut by 27 percent between FY [Fiscal Year] 2005 and FY2010 (adjusted for inflation). We expect to see major cuts to federal public health preparedness programs in both FY2011 and 2012. These inconsistencies represent the greatest threats to our ability to respond to a public health catastrophe on the level of the Japan earthquake and tsunami.

We believe a modernized, prepared public health system must address several remaining gaps:

- A Workforce Gap: The National Association of County and City Health Officials reports that we have lost roughly 19 percent of the local health department workforce since 2008. This loss of experience has a staggering impact on preparedness, as workers cannot simply be hired and trained once a disaster strikes.

- A Surge Capacity Gap: Surge capacity—the ability of the medical system to care for a massive influx of patients— requires ongoing planning, funding, and coordination across healthcare, public health, first responder, and private sectors.

- A Surveillance Gap: The nation still lacks an integrated, national approach to biosurveillance, which could significantly improve response capabilities for emergencies.

- Gaps in Medical Countermeasure Development: The research and development of vaccines, antivirals, diagnostics, and other countermeasures is years ahead of where we were during the 2001 anthrax outbreak; yet our ability to spur innovation in these limited-use technologies has been hampered by a lack of stable funding and some breakdowns in program administration.

PAHPA reauthorization represents an opportunity to fill some of these critical gaps. As you begin consideration of amending the law, TFAH would like to offer the following recommendations:

Strengthen Public Health Preparedness Infrastructure

The economic recession has led to cuts in public health staffing and eroded the basic capabilities of state and local health departments. Strengthening the public health preparedness workforce and infrastructure is critical to ensuring the health protection of our nation. It also requires adequate funding and human resources to recruit and train personnel, stockpile life saving countermeasures, develop and exercise plans, and identify and engage partners to support the public health mission. The resources required to truly modernize public health systems must be made available to bring public health into the 21st century and improve preparedness.

The PHEP cooperative agreements and HPP are two key grant programs that support the development and sustainability of state and local public health preparedness infrastructure. Since their inception, these programs have increased the capacity of state and local health departments and health systems to prepare for and respond to a disaster. Our 2010 report found that these funding streams have contributed to major progress in workforce training, epidemiology and laboratory capacity, surveillance, and planning and exercising at the state and local level.

During the 2009–2010 H1N1 influenza outbreak, state and local health departments were on the front lines responding to the pandemic, though many were limited in their efforts as a result of federal and state budget cuts, particularly those that have occurred over the past five years. These budget crises demonstrated, among other things, the need to build in mechanisms to allow more flexibility in how staff, funded by federal grant programs, are used during emergencies. In the H1N1 influenza response, the ability to re-assign staff from other federally-funded projects in health departments could have improved the financial and human resource efficiencies of that agency's response to the influenza pandemic, especially during the earlier response phases when additional funding was not yet available and jurisdictions needed to mobilize "all hands on deck." To address these concerns, we recommend language that would:

- Establish multi-year grant cycles with greater flexibility in states' retention and use of carry forward and unexpended funds;
- Create a mechanism to fast track the awarding and programming of emergency supplemental funds into existing grant mechanisms without additional match or maintenance of funding requirements; and
- Grant authority to the Secretary to allow states to also use personnel that are part of other federal programs in response to a public health emergency (e.g. an "all hands on deck" scenario).
- We understand that HHS [Health and Human Services] and the Department of Homeland Security (DHS) have begun working to align grant programs that aim to build our nation's emergency preparedness capacity, including PHEP, HPP, and FEMA [Federal Emergency Management

Agency] grants. Currently the PHEP and HPP grants, both of which are often distributed through public health departments, have separate application and reporting requirements, overarching goals, and in some cases conflicting performance metrics. We believe the alignment process should include coordinating grant priorities and goals, grant cycles, and streamlining application and reporting mechanisms to achieve maximum efficiency. I urge you to use PAHPA to ensure oversight and proper implementation of this alignment process.

Modernize Biosurveillance

Situational awareness—knowing what the threats are, and knowing what our capacity to respond is, at any given moment—is critical to responding to any emergency and we need to make sure we are building capacity using 21st century technology and approaches. We have built our disease surveillance system one disease at a time and one crisis at a time, rather than as a unified, interoperable unit. Rather than continuing these silos, we have the opportunity to think across diseases (infectious and chronic) and emergency situations, because health information technology is advancing at a rapid pace and the health care system is becoming electronic.

It is time for public health to do the same. Imagine a system where a provider inputs data into an electronic health record, the health department is rapidly informed of a cluster of unusual symptoms (indicating an outbreak), and the health department then communicates with the provider and responds quickly with the appropriate intervention. Right now, the ability of health departments to receive and analyze electronic data varies widely from jurisdiction to jurisdiction. Because the federal government is in the process of catalyzing adoption of electronic health records, now is the time to think about how to incorporate public health into the system. PAHPA can help fill this gap:

- PAHPA should call for a new national strategy, led
by HHS and CDC [Centers for Disease Control and
Prevention], that would examine means to achieve interoperability and transparency among various surveillance systems. The United States lacks an integrated,
national approach to biosurveillance, and there are major
variations in how quickly states collect and report data
which hamper bioterrorism and disease outbreak response
capabilities. The lack of an overarching federal biosurveillance strategy has led to fragmentation, multiple separate
surveillance systems, and barriers to relevant agencies
prioritizing and synthesizing data. And according to a
December 2010 GAO report, HHS had not provided a
strategic plan for electronic situational awareness, as required by PAHPA.
- The national strategy should also call for leveraging of new
epidemiological data that may become available as a result
of the development of health information technology (IT)
and electronic health records (EHRs). There is no overarching coordination between public health surveillance
efforts at HHS and the work of the Office of the National
Coordinator for Health Information Technology (ONC).
The ONC should work closely with a designated person
at CDC and with state/local/tribal/territorial partners,
with PAHPA mandating this synchronization and collaboration. For example, as ONC develops new standards
for meaningful use of health IT, it should incorporate
the preparedness and biosurveillance implications of
such technologies. Interoperability between public health
and EHRs could not only help with early detection of an
emerging disease outbreak or bioterror attack, but could
also help with identification of targeted populations or
geographic regions to receive medical countermeasures
[MCM] and tracking the post-dispensing impact of medical interventions.

Improve Vaccine and Pharmaceutical Research, Development, and Manufacturing

The United States is falling behind in its research and development of medical countermeasures to fight public health threats. As the nation revamps its approach to research and development of vaccines, medicines, diagnostics and equipment to respond to emerging public health threats, policymakers must ensure public health is involved throughout the process, from initial investment through distribution and dispensing. PAHPA can advance the nation's MCM enterprise through the following activities:

- Congress should consider authorizing President's requests for MCM advancement: building an MCM Strategic Investor to leverage private capital for promising technologies; using unspent H1N1 money to establish Centers for Innovation in Advanced Development and Manufacturing; and developing end-to-end leadership to see products through from initial research through dispensing. However, bill language should request additional detail from HHS on how these programs would be implemented, including multiyear professional judgment budgets for implementation of the PHEMCE [Public Health Emergency Medical Counter-Measures Enterprise] strategy.

- Report language in PAHPA should urge 1) increased coordination between FDA [Food and Drug Administration], BARDA [Biomedical Advanced Research and Development Authority], NIH [National Institute of Health], and CDC from initial investment through dispensing; 2) improved transparency of the development process, including regulatory pathways by FDA and contracting process with BARDA and Bioshield; and 3) MCM strategy should be end-to-end—not just focused on initial investments, but on advance development, procurement, distribution, and surveillance.

- Improving SNS Management: There should be a plan for stocking the Strategic National Stockpile (SNS) and for ongoing replacement of expiring product, especially vaccines, pediatric doses of antimicrobials, antivirals and other products, and restocking matériel used as a result of the H1N1 outbreak. This plan should also include a professional judgment budget for replacing product expiring over the next several years. The legislation should also call for increased coordination between CDC and BARDA on SNS procurement and management.

- Authorize extension of the Shelf-Life Extension Program (SLEP) to state stockpiles of medical matériel. Currently, only federally-held stockpiles are eligible for the SLEP, which can be a cost-effective way to maintain state and local supplies.

Enhance Surge Capacity

In the event of a major disease outbreak or attack, the public health and health care systems would be severely overstretched. Policymakers must address the ability of the health care system to quickly expand beyond normal services during a major emergency. Investments in research and development, stockpiling, and practice in drills and tabletop exercises will aid in the timely distribution of antivirals and other equipment during an outbreak. PAHPA should facilitate health care preparedness by:

- Encouraging enhancements in the Hospital Preparedness Program (HPP). The HPP, administered by the Assistant Secretary for Preparedness and Response (ASPR), aims to prepare the nation's health system for the medical and logistical impacts of a disaster. Rather than continuing to fund individual hospitals for preparing for a crisis, HPP has played a role in spurring creation of regional healthcare coalitions, alliances between hospitals, public health, and emergency management. These coalitions allow for a shared burden and reduce surge to any single facility. However, in many regions, this is still a nascent process. Building and developing these coalitions should be an explicit goal of HPP, including expanding coalitions to every city and linking them into a national system.

- Clarifying crisis standards of care. The federal government should provide a national framework to guide states and local entities in developing crisis standards for use during a mass casualty event. Leaving this process up to the states has not led to enough progress in developing a better understanding of the kind of care that would be available in a disaster.

- Clarifying federal volunteer liability laws to implement one blanket liability that applies to all volunteer health professionals and entities volunteering under a nationally-declared public health emergency or disaster. HHS has acknowledged that a patchwork of federal liability laws is confusing and frustrating to providers. There should also be Federal Tort Claims Act protection for Medical Reserve Corps volunteers year-round, as these personnel participate in public health drills and training during times of non-disaster.

Thank you for this opportunity to weigh in as the Committee considers reauthorization of PAHPA. I look forward to your questions.

Periodical and Internet Sources Bibliography

The following articles have been selected to supplement the diverse views presented in this chapter.

Lee Black	"Informed Consent in the Military: The Anthrax Vaccination Case," *Virtual Mentor*, October 2007.
Ellen Gabler	"Caution Flag Raised on Mandatory Anthrax Vaccines," *JSOnline*, October 29, 2007.
Anthony Gucciardi	"Children May Be Given Death-Linked Anthrax Shots Under Bioterrorism Scare Trials," InfoWars.com, October 26, 2011.
James G. Hodge, Lawrence O. Gostin, and Jon S. Vernick	"The Pandemic and All-Hazards Preparedness Act Improving Public Health Emergency Response," *JAMA*, April 18, 2007.
Stephen Lendman	"Readying Americans for Dangerous, Mandatory Vaccinations," Mathaba.com, June 10, 2009.
Stuart L. Nightingale, Joanna M. Prasher, and Stewart Simonson	"Emergency Use Authorization (EUA) to Enable Use of Needed Products in Civilian and Military Emergencies, United States," *Emerging Infectious Diseases*, July 2007.
Steven Salzberg	"The Anthrax Vaccine Boondoggle," *Forbes*, October 30, 2011.
Rob Stein	"Possible Study of Anthrax Vaccine's Effectiveness in Children Stirs Debate," *Washington Post*, October 24, 2011.
Bob Unruh	"Citizens Could Be Facing Mandatory Anthrax Shots," *WorldNetDaily*, April 4, 2007.
Julie Weisberg	"Pentagon Conducting Research into Adverse Effects of Anthrax Vaccine While Maintaining It Is Safe," *Raw Story*, March 27, 2007.

For Further Discussion

Chapter 1

1. The Scientists Working Group on Biological and Chemical Weapons contends that the focus on bioterrorism has diverted resources and attention from the threat of infectious diseases. The Bipartisan WMD Terrorism Research Center, however, maintains that an enemy armed with an engineered pathogen is a greater threat. In your view, which author provides the most compelling argument? Use examples from the viewpoints to support your answer.

2. The Department of Agriculture's Office of Inspector General states that large-scale contamination of the US food supply is a serious threat given the nation's experience with unintentional outbreaks of foodborne illnesses. Do you agree or disagree with the author? Why or why not?

3. R. Goodrich Schneider et al. suggest that agroterrorism has great potential to disrupt the farming industry. On the other hand, Mary Zanoni insists that droughts and dwindling resources are more urgent issues for agriculture. In your opinion, which author provides the most persuasive position? Refer to examples in the texts to explain your response.

Chapter 2

1. Kenneth King claims that high-containment laboratories increase the risks of accidental outbreaks and unauthorized access to pathogens. In your opinion, does the Committee on Special Immunizations Program for Laboratory Personnel Engaged in Research on Countermeasures for Select Agents successfully address this concern? Why or why not?

2. Nancy Kingsbury points out that no federal agency has been designated to oversee the proliferation of high-containment

laboratories. In your view, does Hugh Auchincloss offer a convincing response to this concern? Use examples from the viewpoints to support your answer.

3. The Biological Weapons Prevention Project asserts that citizens' concerns are ignored in the decision-making of biodefense research. In your opinion, which author in the chapter pays the least attention to local communities? Refer to examples in the texts to explain your response.

Chapter 3

1. In your opinion, would Laura Meckler's description of the bioterror drills performed in Tucson, Arizona, make the public feel more or less confident about the country's preparedness for a bioterrorist attack? Why or why not?

2. *Newsweek* proposes that mass vaccination would be more effective than selective ring vaccination in the case of a smallpox attack. Fred Hutchinson Cancer Research Center, nonetheless, supports ring vaccination rather than mass vaccination. In your view, which author presents the most realistic evidence? Use examples from the viewpoints to support your answer.

3. Richard J. Danzig, Rachel Kleinfeld, and Philipp C. Bleek state that bioterrorism preparedness treats citizens more as problems than as solutions. Do you agree or disagree with the authors? Why or why not?

Chapter 4

1. Eric S. Morse touts the developments in bioterrorism countermeasures under Project BioShield, while Jon Cohen weighs the policy's failures. Considering the evidence from both authors, in your opinion, is Project BioShield an overall success or failure? Use examples from the viewpoints to support your answer.

2. MILVAX maintains that anthrax vaccinations for the military are a success if they lead adversaries to switch to other biological weapons that are less of a threat. Do you agree or disagree with the author? Why or why not?

Organizations to Contact

The editors have compiled the following list of organizations concerned with the issues debated in this book. The descriptions are derived from materials provided by the organizations. All have publications or information available for interested readers. The list was compiled on the date of publication of the present volume; names, addresses, phone and fax numbers, and e-mail and Internet addresses may change. Be aware that many organizations take several weeks or longer to respond to inquiries, so allow as much time as possible.

Association of State and Territorial Health Officials (ASTHO)
2231 Crystal Drive, Suite 450
Arlington, VA 22202
(202) 371-9090 • fax: (571) 527-3189
website: http://astho.org

ASTHO is a national nonprofit organization representing the state and territorial public health agencies of the United States, US Territories, and District of Columbia. ASTHO works to formulate and influence sound public health policy, particularly regarding bioterrorism preparedness. The organization publishes newsletters, survey results, resource lists, and policy papers that assist states in the development of bioterrorism preparedness and other policies.

Bipartisan WMD Terrorism Research Center
1747 Pennsylvania Avenue NW, Suite 700
Washington, DC 20006
website: www.wmdcenter.org

The WMD Center is a nonprofit research and education organization founded by members of the Congressional Commission on the Prevention of Weapons of Mass Destruction Proliferation and Terrorism in 2010. The center's goals are to improve capability to respond to bioterrorism to a degree that, in effect, removes bioterrorism from the category of weapons of mass destruction; strengthen overall public health and medical care delivery systems to respond to a wide range of natural and man-made disasters; and keep the United States on the leading edge of the biotechnical revolution. It publishes the *Bio-Response Report Card*.

Bradford Disarmament Research Center
University of Bradford
Bradford, West Yorkshire BD7 1DP
United Kingdom
44 (0)1274 23 2323
e-mail: course-enquiries@bradford.ac.uk
website: www.brad.ac.uk/acad/bdrc

The Bradford Disarmament Research Center Department of Peace Studies is an international center of academic and policy-oriented research on the proliferation and control of nuclear, biological, chemical and conventional weapons. The center administers the Biological and Toxin Weapons Convention (BTWC) website, opbw.org, which provides up-to-date information about the BTWC. It also publishes various research reports and studies on biological, chemical, and nuclear disarmament.

Center for Arms Control and Nonproliferation
322 4th Street NE
Washington, DC 20002
(202) 546-0795 • fax: (202) 546-5142
website: http://armscontrolcenter.org

The Center for Arms Control and Nonproliferation is a nonprofit, nonpartisan policy organization that is dedicated to enhancing international peace and security and protecting American people from the threat of weapons of mass destruction. It seeks to reduce and ultimately eliminate nuclear weapons and halt the spread of all weapons of mass destruction, including biological weapons. Staff at the organization provide commentary and analysis published in newspapers and journals throughout the world.

The Center for Biosecurity of UPMC
The Pier IV Building
621 E. Pratt Street, Suite 210
Baltimore, MD 21202
(443) 573-3304 • fax: (443) 573-3305
website: www.upmc-biosecurity.org

The Center for Biosecurity is an independent, nonprofit organization of the University of Pittsburgh Medical Center (UPMC). The center works to change public policy in order to lessen the illness, death, and civil disruption that would follow a large-scale biological attack or a natural epidemic. It publishes several journals, including *Biosecurity and Bioterrorism, Clinicians' Biosecurity News*, and *Biosecurity News Today.*

Centers for Disease Control and Prevention (CDC)
1600 Clifton Road
Atlanta, GA 30333
(800) 232-4636 (CDC-INFO)
e-mail: cdcinfo@cdc.gov
website: www.cdc.gov

The CDC is the main health agency of the US government. The mission of the CDC is to promote health and quality of life by preventing and controlling disease, injury, and disability. The CDC provides up-to-date information to the public on health and diseases. The agency publishes several journals including *Emerging Infectious Diseases* and *Morbidity and Mortality Weekly Report.*

Defense Science Board (DSB)
The Pentagon, OUSD (AT&L)
Room 3C553
Washington, DC 20310

(703) 695-4157

website: www.acq.osd.mil/dsb

The DSB, created by the US government in 1956, seeks to use newly acquired scientific knowledge and technologies in order to help defend the United States against enemy attacks. The board, comprised of US scientists, advises the US Department of Defense (DoD) on ways to defend the US against biological, chemical, and nuclear warfare and helps to ensure the DoD takes advantage of revolutionary new technologies. The DSB publishes a quarterly newsletter and various in-depth reports.

Department of Homeland Security (DHS)

245 Murray Lane SW

Washington, DC 20528-0075

(202) 282-8000

website: www.dhs.gov

Formed in response to the September 11, 2001 terrorist attacks, the DHS is a consolidation of twenty-two federal agencies. The department's mission is to ensure a homeland that is safe, secure, and resilient against terrorism and other hazards, supported by more than 240,000 employees—from aviation and border security to emergency response and from cybersecurity analysts to chemical facility inspectors. With the Centers for Disease Control and Prevention (CDC), the DHS operates the Strategic National Stockpile (SNS), a repository of countermeasures and medical supplies for terrorist attacks and national emergencies.

Federation of American Scientists (FAS)

1725 DeSales Street NW, 6th Floor

Washington, DC 20036

(202) 546-3300 • fax: (202) 675-1010

e-mail: fas@fas.org

website: www.fas.org

FAS is an international, nonprofit organization comprised of scientists and engineers who promote humanitarian uses of science and technology. FAS seeks to provide the public, media, and policy makers with high-quality information to better inform debates about science-related issues, including the proliferation of biological weapons. The organization publishes a variety of material including the *FAS Public Interest Report* and *Terrorism Analysis Reports*.

Henry L. Stimson Center
1111 19th Street, 12th Floor
Washington, DC 20036
(202) 223-5956 • fax: (202) 238-9604
e-mail: webmaster@stimson.org
website: www.stimson.org

The Henry L. Stimson Center is a nonprofit, nonpartisan institution devoted to enhancing international peace and security through analysis and outreach. It focuses on reducing weapons of mass destruction, strengthening institutions for international peace and security, and building regional security. The center publishes various books, reports, commentaries, and background papers.

Military Vaccine (MILVAX) Agency
(877) 438-8222 (GET-VACC) • fax: (703) 428-0177
e-mail: vaccines@amedd.army.mil
website: www.vaccines.mil

Located in northern Virginia, MILVAX supports Department of Defense (DoD) vaccination programs protecting military service members, their dependents, and beneficiaries as well as provides educational support and training resources for DoD healthcare providers and clinicians. Its website offers information on a range of vaccines and diseases, education toolkits, and other resources.

National Institute of Allergy and Infectious Diseases (NIAID)

Office of Communications and Public Liaison
6610 Rockledge Drive, MSC 6612
Bethesda, MD 20892-6612
(866) 284-4107 • fax: (301) 402-3573
website: www.niaid.nih.gov

NIAID is an agency within the US Department of Health and Human Services. It conducts and supports basic and applied research to better understand, treat, and prevent infectious, immunologic, and allergic diseases. The agency issues several publications, briefs, and reports on infectious diseases and biodefense.

World Health Organization (WHO)

Avenue Appia 20
1211 Geneva 27, Switzerland
41 22 791 2111 • fax: 41 22 791 3111
e-mail: info@who.int
website: www.who.int

WHO is the directing and coordinating authority for health within the United Nations system. It is responsible for providing leadership on global health matters, shaping the health research agenda, setting norms and standards, articulating evidence-based policy options, providing technical support to countries, and monitoring and assessing health trends.

Bibliography of Books

Lawrence Archer and Fiona Bawdon

Ricin!: The Inside Story of the Terror Plot That Never Was. New York: Pluto Press, 2010.

Michael Christopher Carroll

Lab 257: The Disturbing Story of the Government's Secret Plum Island Germ Laboratory. New York: Morrow, 2004.

William R. Clark

Bracing for Armageddon?: The Science and Politics of Bioterrorism in America. New York: Oxford University Press, 2008.

Anne Clunan, Peter R. Lavoy, and Susan B. Martin, eds.

Terrorism, War, or Disease?: Unraveling the Use of Biological Weapons. Stanford, CA: Stanford Security Studies, 2008.

Bob Coen and Eric Nadler

Dead Silence: Fear and Terror on the Anthrax Trail. Berkeley, CA: Counterpoint, 2009.

Leonard A. Cole

The Anthrax Letters: A Bioterrorism Expert Investigates the Attacks That Shocked America. New York: Skyhorse, 2009.

Sari Edelstein, Bonnie Gerald, Tamara Crutchley Bushell, and Craig Gundersen

Food Nutrition and Risk in America: Food Insecurity, Biotechnology, Food Safety, and Bioterrorism. New York: Jones and Bartlett, 2009.

David P. Fidler and Lawrence O. Gostin	*Biosecurity in the Global Age: Biological Weapons, Public Health, and the Rule of Law.* Stanford, CA: Stanford Law and Politics, 2008.
I.W. Fong and Kenneth Alibek, eds.	*Bioterrorism and Infectious Agents: A New Dilemma for the 21st Century.* New York: Springer, 2009.
Stephen J. Forsythe	*The Microbiology of Safe Food,* 2nd ed. Ames, IA: Blackwell, 2010.
Jeanne Guillemin	*American Anthrax: Fear, Crime, and the Investigation of the Nation's Deadliest Bioterror Attack.* New York: Time Books, 2011.
R. William Johnstone	*Bioterror: Anthrax, Influenza, and the Future of Public Health Security.* Westport, CT: Praeger Security International, 2008.
Susan D. Jones	*Death in a Small Package: A Short History of Anthrax.* Baltimore, MD: Johns Hopkins University Press, 2010.
Barry Kellman	*Bioviolence: Preventing Biological Terror and Crime.* New York: Cambridge University Press, 2007.
Gregory D. Koblentz	*Living Weapons: Biological Warfare and International Security.* Ithaca, NY: Cornell University Press, 2009.

| Jeffrey A. Lockwood | *Six-Legged Soldiers: Using Insects as Weapons of War.* New York: Oxford University Press, 2009. |

| Shawn B. McNeill, ed. | *Bioterrorism: Biosurveillance, Project Bioshield, and Other Countermeasures.* New York: Nova Science, 2010. |

| Don Nardo | *Invisible Weapons: The Science of Biological and Chemical Warfare.* Mankato, MN: Compass Point Books, 2011. |

| Jennifer T. Ollington, ed. | *Agro-Terrorism.* New York: Nova Science Publishers, 2008. |

| Kedar N. Prasad | *Bio-Shield: Antioxidants Against Radiological, Chemical, and Biological Weapons.* New York: Strategic Book Publishing, 2008. |

| Edward M. Spiers | *A History of Chemical and Biological Weapons.* London, UK: Reaction, 2010. |

| Jonathan B. Tucker | *Innovation, Dual Use, and Security: Managing the Risks of Emerging Biological and Chemical Technologies.* Cambridge, MA: MIT Press, 2012. |

| Mark Wheelis, Lajos Rózsa, and Malcolm Dando, eds. | *Deadly Cultures: Biological Weapons Since 1945.* Cambridge, MA: Harvard University Press, 2006. |

David Willman *The Mirage Man: Bruce Ivins, the Anthrax Attacks, and America's Rush to War.* New York: Bantam Books, 2011.

Index

Influenza A (H1N1), 34, 135, 198
Influenza pandemics
  deaths from, 21, 32, 111
  preparedness for, 149
  threat from, 111–112, 115–116
Insecticide contamination, 41
Institute of Medicine (IOM), 190, 193
Institutional Biosafety Committees (IBCs), 98–99
International Science and Technology Center, 187
Iran, 16
Iraq, 89, 180–181
Ivins, Bruce, 192

J

Japan
  air-dropped torpedoes by, 23
  anthrax use by, 179
  Aum Shinrikyo cult in, 26, 31, 49, 180
  banning beef in, 44
  smallpox research in, 15
Jenkins, Brian Michael, 50
Jenner, Edward, 71, 79n1
Jolley, Chuck, 62–65
Jones, Vernon, 131

K

Kaczynski, Ted, 27
Kadlec, Robert, 170, 172, 177
Keim, Paul, 68
King, Kenneth, 80–91
Kingsbury, Nancy, 101–109
Kleinfeld, Rachel, 148–156
Klotz, Lynn C., 109–117
Koch, Robert, 71, 79n1
Kurilla, Michel, 171, 176

L

Large-animal veterinarian shortage, 65

Larsen, Randy, 135
Lederberg, Joshua, 24
Lieberman, Joe, 163
Longini, Ira M., 143, 145–146
Lyme disease, 21

M

Mad cow disease. *See* Bovine spongiform encephalopathy (BSE)
Malaysia, 24
Marburg virus, 33, 83
Marijuana eradication, 48
Mass vaccinations
  needed against smallpox, 14, 137–141
  not needed against smallpox, 142–147
Material threat assessment, 174
McConnell, Mitch, 163
McVeigh, Timothy, 87
Meckler, Laura, 129–133
Medical Countermeasure Development, 199
Medical countermeasures (MCMs), 159–160, 202
Medical Reserve Corps, 205
Medical surge capacity
  enhancing, 204
  funding for, 116
  gap, 198
  improving, 35, 150, 152, 155
Meliodosis, 87
Methicillin-resistant *Staphylococcus aureus* (MRSA), 32, 111
Metropolitan Medical Response System, 131
Mexico, 48
Military Vaccine (MILVAX) Agency, 178–188
Mission Oriented Protective Posture (MOPP), 185